Alexandra Stoddard's

LIVING

BEAUTIFULLY

TOGETHER

Books by Alexandra Stoddard

Alexandra Stoddard's

LIVING
BEAUTIFULLY
TOGETHER

BY ALEXANDRA STODDARD

DOUBLEDAY

NEW YORK LONDON TORONTO SYDNEY AUCKLAND

Lines from *The Prophet*, by Kahlil Gibran, are
quoted with the permission of Alfred A. Knopf, Inc.
Copyright 1923 by Kahlil Gibran, renewed 1951 by
Administrator C.T.A. of Kahlil Gibran Estate and
Mary G. Gibran.

PUBLISHED BY DOUBLEDAY
a division of Bantam Doubleday Dell Publishing Group, Inc.
666 Fifth Avenue, New York, New York 10103

DOUBLEDAY and the portrayal of an anchor with a dolphin
are trademarks of Doubleday, a division of
Bantam Doubleday Dell Publishing Group, Inc.

Library of Congress Cataloging-in-Publication Data

Stoddard, Alexandra.
Living beautifully together / by Alexandra Stoddard.—1st ed.
p.   cm.
ISBN 0-385-24777-X
1. Conduct of life.   I. Title.
BJ1581.2.S755   1989   88-25745
158′.2—dc19   CIP

FOR JOHN BOWEN COBURN
WHO MARRIED PETER AND ME
AND WHO HELPS THOUSANDS OF PEOPLE
LIVE BEAUTIFULLY TOGETHER BY HIS GRACE,
FRIENDSHIP, SPIRIT AND LOVE.

Acknowledgments

*To Nancy Evans and
Sally Arteseros, whose
vision, wisdom, and
inspiration added
immeasurably to this
book.*

THANK YOU

*To Kate Medina and Carl
Brandt, who have
believed in me
from the beginning
of my journey.*

THANK YOU

Contents

Contents

Preface

"Love is best."
—*Robert Browning*

I'd like to think of this book as a process. In my work as an interior designer, I've had the opportunity to share thoughts and ideas with hundreds of clients and friends—we have explored insights and ways we can live beautifully together. I hope this book will give you and me the opportunity to think out loud as we look for ways to bring more beauty and meaning into our lives.

I love beginnings! As I begin to write this book, I feel I know many of you who read *Living a Beautiful Life* and reached out in loving ways to me. I'm forever enriched and renewed by your wonderful handwritten letters and personal stories. So many of you have shared your views and appreciations with me, sent me tapes, notepaper, poetry, and books—all these gracious, generous, loving acts inspire me to continue my search with fresh inspiration. I am grateful and thank you most sincerely.

Living a Beautiful Life was about how to enjoy each day, not saving our living for a special 5 percent of the time. It was about how to create rituals so we can savor our lives. Now I want to turn to the subject of how we can enrich our lives daily with one another.

Each of us is going through a private search for more beauty and meaning in our lives. The way we learn to seek answers is by loving the world that made us. When we take care to nurture our own spirit, this self-nurturing is the springboard from which we bounce outward toward the world. When you and I feel love and contentment in our hearts, invariably we want to reach out to somebody else. Love, received, triggers us to pass it on and connect through some loving gesture. Love shared always expands us.

Clearly the world at the end of the twentieth century has gone a bit mad. Cicero said, "Philosophers apply the term sickness to all disturbances of the soul." Everywhere we look we see a world out of control. But maybe we can become a little more conscious of who we are and where we fit into this world. We can make a greater effort to be generous and loving and to value ourselves, our families and friends. Now that we have discovered that mere acquisition just gets you things, not satisfaction or joy—that things can later become burdensome—we can spend more time appreciating the gifts we have and not dwell on what we don't have. Deep, abiding, authentic relationships, in which we live beautifully among others in a loving manner, will sustain us to the end.

We all need material goods and when used properly they can indeed benefit us and others. Since the beginning of recorded history it has been a sign of civilized people that they live as attractively as they can and as comfortably as they can within the framework of what they can afford. We want to live graciously and we want to share our full, committed lives with others. Living beautifully together is an art that takes time to learn as well as time to enjoy.

Nothing of value comes quickly. Everything is a great deal easier, however, if we open up and know ourselves better by letting our defenses down, understanding that we are all equally vulnerable. Life can be far more enjoyable when we can grow to be more lovable—first to ourselves and then to others. If we can know that our best is the most that we have to give—and no airs or pretensions or outside trappings can improve the real core of our being—we

Prize the moment.

will remain humble and sincere. We should continuously work on reaching our essence because it is there where we exude love and can become lovable.

The difficult struggles we've all experienced—our losses—are our muscle and strength. We learn through loss not to hold on too tightly. It is the nature of living that we will all lose what we have. Why can't we then hold on to what we have at the moment and not dwell on loss when it occurs? Losses help give us our special courage to face the future with excitement and optimism, knowing we have to live and love now. "One must put all the happiness one can into each moment." Edith Wharton expressed this thought in a love letter to William Morton Fullerton in 1908. Today, right now, continuously work at filling your well with a love of life so that even on sour days you can draw from it and it will never be empty. Keep moving, prevail, and work toward your beliefs.

Use your life's capital as your unequaled gift. Do all you can to contribute something uniquely yours to the world, something that only you can give. Search inside yourself for what you are most passionate about and how you can share this with others so that your life's process will have a real purpose. You can feel satisfied that in your own way, on your own terms in the times in which you live, your life has far greater meaning and beauty than you even dare dream. When you feel this in abundance, you will be capable of living beautifully with others. Your spirit is then able to enliven the spirit inside those you know and love and those you want to know and love.

Scatter joy.

—RALPH WALDO EMERSON

Part One

NOURISHING YOURSELF

I've discovered that the best way to live a beautiful life with others is to begin by cultivating yourself. When you take good care of yourself, you free yourself to enjoy healthy relationships with others, and one of life's great opportunities is affirming the dignity and greatness in others. There is a direct relationship between how well we can learn to love others and how well we love ourselves. People, like newborn babies and gardens, need nurturing. I used to think that we were meant to love and give to others and that they, in return, would love and give to us. But I've grown to realize that is not the way it works.

Each of us must become impassioned, finding meaning and self-fulfillment in our own life's journey. We must mature to become dependent on ourselves, not on others, to take care of us. To discover this truth makes us free. I think of self-nurturing as a flame. Once we have a flame we can pass it on and light other people's torches. Your original flame is never diminished. This fire, this strength and courage, comes from deep inside each of us and becomes our gift to ourselves and others. The way we can share this inner light and energy is by living a full, happy life which we find exciting, challenging, and beautiful.

If we have self-esteem, it has been hard earned. When we find life a positive adventure, we know firsthand how wonderful it can be when we learn how to take charge of ourselves. We can radiate enthusiasm toward others because it is the outward symbol of our inner vision. When we have something of value to give, it is bursting for a creative outlet. When we are passionate we have a need to share this excitement with others. We feel so good inside, we burst with energy and enthusiasm and want to spread the good news. A personal commitment to find life uniquely meaningful takes a certain kind of courage. You have to discover all the possibilities available to you, be open to change, and take risks as you chart a new world. Think of yourself as holding a key in your hand, a key you possess that unlocks doors for you, opening your world to more beauty and possibility. You do possess this key. Use it. Work hard to open as many doors as possible. Some you will want to close, and others you will want to keep open; you may want to invite other people inside.

If we don't make the extra effort to treat ourselves well, we have no experience of the depth of possibilities open to us for sharing our best selves with others. Begin by nurturing your soul, mind, body, and spirit before you reach out to others. Nurture your soul by meditation—your personal style might be to walk in the woods or along a beach or in a garden. Regularly feed your essence by reflection and contemplation, prayer and reading. Decide what is the most fun way for you to keep your body fit and make a commitment to yourself to a regular weekly exercise regimen: Dance, swim, ride a bike, or play tennis. Take time to nurture your spirit by going to an art museum, writing, painting, or studying. Select several classics you haven't read and make a reading list for yourself with a schedule so you make time to enrich your mind. All these things are essential for us to remain balanced. Everything that will ever be constructive and good in our relationships depends on how well we follow the simple instruction, "To thine own self be true." There is nothing narcissistic about caring for yourself when others depend on you. Yet all too often we forget this and

Take an hour a day for yourself.

feel guilty doing what has become the essential first step toward living beautifully with others.

CIVILITY

The universal theme in religions and philosophies appears to be a version of the Golden Rule: "Do unto others as you would have them do unto you." Human beings have a deep desire to be kind to others. Yet we find it difficult to be kind when we feel out of kilter ourselves. When you treat someone else badly it is always because you treat yourself badly. When, in turn, you treat someone else beautifully it is a mirror reflecting how you treat yourself. In order to get along well in the world and be thoughtful toward others, we have to know firsthand how to listen, be kind, be courteous and civilized to ourselves.

BEING PERSONALLY RESPONSIBLE

We might have all good intentions to please our partners, care for our children, honor our parents, nurture friends, serve bosses, and be helpful to co-workers, but if we become overwhelmed we're of no use to anyone.

Realistically, no one can ever be there for us twenty-four hours a day. Nor can we be there for anyone else every second of the day. We are mature in direct relationship to how well we handle ourselves in the ups and downs of life on our own. We will be challenged when we least expect it. So we have to be prepared by strengthening our inner resources. Strength and courage can't be faked and we will constantly be tested. One day I came back from lunch and found two phone messages: a best friend's apartment had been badly burned in a fire, and my brother had called to tell me our father died of a heart attack. I hopped in a taxi and went to my friend whose apartment had just burned up. I knew there was nothing I could do for my father and I could help my friend and her small baby get settled in a neighbor's apartment. I was glad to be able to be useful and it helped me work through my loss in a positive, constructive way.

Through facing reality we know that horrible things do happen to good and innocent people. We learn through our own experiences that often what happens to us is not as important as how well we react and grow from what happens to us.

Nurture yourself each day so that you will naturally respond to other people's needs and losses in a helpful way. One way I nurture myself is by writing in my journal every day. I love to come home from work and take a long bubble bath before I do anything domestic or constructive. My mood immediately elevates and once I've pampered myself and had time alone, then I'm ready to enjoy whatever the evening activities may be. I have a room I like to retreat to where I listen to music and putter. I like to look through books and clip out articles from magazines. I make time to do these things because they bring me grace. I set my alarm clock early enough for me to have a minimum of one hour to myself in the morning before the day clicks into high gear. I need time to reflect and be alone when I'm free to do whatever the spirit moves me to do.

No one can give us these gifts of private time but ourselves. Take them. Cling to them. Make your own time as sacred as time spent with others. When my daughters Alexandra and Brooke were young I got up at five every morning so that I could first nurture myself: I'd write until six-thirty, then read the paper and have coffee until seven when they awoke. I was happy to nurture them before giving them breakfast and taking them to school and going to my office. If I don't get a jump on the day I end up with my equilibrium out of balance. Recently I was putting in late nights writing and we had experienced horrible weather. The alarm went off one Tuesday morning at six and it was so dark and dreary I went back to sleep until eight and, because I didn't have any morning appointments, I stayed at home and wrote in bed. What a difference this made to my mood!

We have to recondition our thinking and understand that all

Inner strength requires time alone.

the good we do depends on continuously nurturing our own spirits. Instead of feeling guilty or lazy when I feed my spirit, I feel useless and ashamed when I am too scattered to care for myself properly.

When you keep your spirit healthy, you will be spontaneously ready to console others. Not seeking to be consoled, you are living as beautifully as possible. The key is to nurture your own soul so you avoid any degree of self-pity, no matter how great your own problems may be.

Living beautifully with ourselves and others requires gaining control and power over the things we *can* change, maximizing the positive things, appreciating without guilt all the good, and minimizing the negatives. That may seem like a tall order, but it is in our control by what we do in all our small acts each day. And we are constantly reinforced by how much better we feel about ourselves, our relationships, and our daily lives. So we begin where we are, by getting all the parts of our lives working together smoothly so we're free to move forward. Maybe you need to organize your house or apartment so that it runs more efficiently. If your clothes closet is set up so that you can see everything at a glance, you will enjoy your wardrobe more and also the process of dressing and undressing. Or maybe you need to arrange your books by author so you know where all your books are for easy reference. If you feel tension in your house with your cleaning woman you should probably make a change. If your decorator doesn't listen well and you are frustrated, explore your options. If there is one thing that's not right, we have to fix it—work through it and go on to new challenges. Harmony requires getting caught up with all the areas of our daily lives so that we gain control.

If we value honesty in ourselves we will seek honesty in our relationships with others. When we discipline ourselves to be dependable, meet our challenges head on, face even the most difficult realities squarely, determine to be strong when we'd rather be weak, we gain uncrushable self-confidence. Security comes from knowing we can handle ourselves beautifully whatever cards are dealt us. Believe in your power to rise above any adversity and you will be given the necessary strength. My mother preached "stick-to-itive-ness" to her four children as a necessary character trait. We were allowed to fail but never to quit. When we nurture an optimistic approach to all we do, we don't just reinforce ourselves, we support and encourage others to live up to their potential. Life is not a question of success or failure, but living well requires doing your best under all circumstances and never making excuses.

I've always admired adventurers, those who reach for the most exhilarating paths, exploring unknown territories, not being satisfied with the safe, bland, manicured zones mapped out by others. I am an explorer of my own life; any other charted course would be entrapping to my spirit. We need to stretch our minds, bodies, souls, and spirits in all we do. I'd rather lose a tennis game 6–0, 6–0 and feel I fought with all my might than easily win an unchallenging match without perspiration. Life is most thrilling when we live intensely. In fact, we tend to become more nervous and stressed when we're afraid to extend ourselves because we know we can dig deeper and perform better. I enjoy being fueled by the right hemisphere of the brain, where the mystery, the intuitive, and the spiritual have a sacred place. I find it exciting to know there will be many surprises in the future and the more I challenge myself, the deeper will be the joys.

Being kind to yourself is not selfish; it is the opposite. Self-kindness is really thoughtful and loving. You nurture a tender, considerate, helping nature which becomes you in all your associations. You are a positive source of energy, goodness and love.

LISTEN TO YOUR FEELINGS   You can never really afford to avoid paying attention to your feelings. Once you make an effort to listen to your own needs regularly, this will become a way of life. Take care of basics as you go along. Leave spaces in your day to do something spontaneous. No matter who you are, you are your own boss for certain times each day. If you work for someone else you may need your lunch hour to do something for yourself. See an exhibition or browse in a bookstore. We can't be with others nonstop without replenishing energy. You don't have to be ill to feel you can cancel an appointment. People are understanding. Recently I canceled a meeting to look for antiques with a client because the weather was foul and I felt I just couldn't keep the appointment and still be myself. My client understood. In fact, she was glad to have a chance to sit at her desk and make a dent in her correspondence. We rescheduled and it proved to be the wiser choice because I would have been grumpy if I hadn't. You can't do a good job for others if you're feeling blue. Don't be hard on yourself, simply work hard. Self-sufficiency, self-respect, efficiency, the discipline of hard work are tools that open doors to a wider vision. Make these a habit and if you have to reschedule an appointment occasionally, think about all the things you accomplished in the new time you made for yourself.

Having a positive frame of mind toward ourselves is a constructive, upbeat way of living beautifully and you must learn how to develop this as though you were learning to ice-skate or drive a car. The key is to understand that when you love your life and your work you radiate this enthusiasm to others. Whenever you pursue your own interests it naturally results in an uplifted spirit.

Celebrate all that is beautiful and poignant.

Some are born with a more natural aptitude than others, just as some are born natural athletes, but all of us can learn useful ways to improve our attitudes. Women have a harder time nurturing themselves because culturally we have been taught to serve others. I have a good friend who has to work at turning a gray day into a positive one. She finds she gets sick of complaining and eventually turns things around by doing something that completely absorbs her. Nancy is an artist and feels torn between her role of wife, mother, hostess, and housekeeper and her need to paint. No matter how difficult a canvas is, she never feels frustrated; instead she feels challenged and becomes lost in the intensity and focus creativity always provides her. When you have developed a self-affirming vision of things, you cease wasting your energy in self-defeating thoughts. Fears and doubts lose their hold as you develop an affirmative nature.

Many of us get stuck because we give in to feelings of guilt which only entrap our spirit from moving forward. Many times we feel guilty because we have neglected to act in a loving, constructive way toward someone. Instead of feeling guilty we can leap into some positive action. Write a note. Send flowers. Call on the phone. Deliver a present. Invite that person to dinner. Send an article you know will be of special interest, or a book. Instead of apologizing and reminding the person how neglectful you've been, be positive and glad to be back in touch.

It is not gracious to remind people how busy you are because it comes across as self-important. If you feel that you're doing the best you can and you will never get fully caught up, then simply begin where you are. Accept your human situation. I go back to my premise that when you spend enough time taking care of yourself you will find the time and have the will to reach out to others. If you find yourself feeling guilty because of the way you have neglected others, think about the way you've treated yourself. Rate each day from one to ten on how well you are nurturing your own spirit. Do you see a parallel with the way you treat others? I always see a direct link in my own life.

Dr. Jane Cowles, a cancer therapist who spent four years as Director of Total Patient Care on a fifty-five-bed cancer unit in Houston before moving to New York, only sees a few private patients now. She explained, "My work was extremely intense and many of our patients died. I tended to neglect myself because I was preoccupied with helping the patients. Our small unit had a full-time psychologist, dietitian, social worker, and physical therapist. We had art classes and other activities in the 'living room,' and the unit became a creative place, dramatizing the human potential and spirit. When I left Texas I felt I left a large part of me there. I felt drained. I knew I had to concentrate on taking care of myself as much as I had cared for those special patients."

Become more aware of yourself. Listen to your body. For instance, I have a sensitive back and whenever I am overly stressed and feel too much pressure I pull my back out. I've done this by brushing my hair, reaching for a sweater, or bending down to pick up some fallen leaves from our ficus trees. I accept the aching back and ease up on my schedule. The pain is a good reminder I've gone too far. I pace myself and spend more unstructured time. I am brutally honest in my journal. Usually I sound like Pollyanna because I love my work and am happy in my life. When I press too hard I exhaust myself and my journal tells me the truth. Pay attention to your spirit. Whenever we get too caught up with the demands of our work we risk becoming dulled and insensitive to both our own needs and the needs of those we love. Ease up on your schedule; have quiet evenings at home when you can curl up in bed and read magazines. Catch a potential problem before it's too late—it will save so much time and energy. Problems never come at convenient times. The old adage "A stitch in time saves nine" is wise and true. I hate waste so severely that I try to avoid it in all areas of my life. But we all get caught off guard at times. When I am behind in my work, I work harder in order to try to catch up. Often I end up with a cold or flu, utterly defeating my best intentions! An artist friend got a lot of publicity recently and I called her to congratulate her on her success. She was in bed with flu, miserable. "I'll never get caught up with myself."

Diagnose yourself immediately before a symptom is allowed to develop into something too big to handle. Cancel a meeting. Close your office door. Shut your eyes. Put your head back and put cotton balls soaked with witch hazel on your eyelids. Listen. Talk to yourself. Tell yourself how you feel. What hurts? Why go to a doctor to learn you need to take it easy for a day? Tell yourself. You know the truth. Remember, if you can tell a doctor you can tell yourself. "Doctor" means "teacher." Teach yourself to be more gentle. It's common sense that gets clouded over when we are overly pressured. Once a family doctor prescribed that I should go to the sun for a few days so my sinuses would clear up and I'd get fresh air and exercise. Now I've learned to do things I love to do that are also good for my health.

SELF-REMEDIES AND PAMPERING

In the clutter and pressure of our stressful and dehumanized technological age, we need to take whatever time is necessary to rediscover the joys of feeling great about our lives. This might mean going on the spur of the moment to get your hair done—which really means getting away from everyone so you can get your senses back. And under the dryer you might feel inspired to write some brief notes to friends using a selection of Joan Brady watercolors reproduced on notepaper. You might want to take a trip alone. You might even decide to sell your house on the lake and free yourself to travel, exploring a variety of different places. Having healthy interpersonal relationships with others depends on our sometimes being unavailable while we give in to necessary self-repairs.

Say "no" to a relative who asks to spend the night—not because you don't have a spare bed but because you need to be free and alone. Dr. John Coburn, the former Bishop of Massachusetts, taught me how to say no. He explained that we become thin in spirit when we are stretched too far. He says no, not based on open spaces in his datebook, but because the voids are necessary so he can fill up his spirit. He says no when he doesn't feel he can put his heart and soul into something.

Walk home or partway home from the office, taking a new route. Look up. Study the trees, the buildings, and the scenery and pretend you are a photographer. Mentally go through rolls of film. Once home, you'll feel transformed. On another trip home, carry a camera and explore the beauty that is there for you to discover.

Try some kindness and vitality on yourself. Get out an exercise mat and spray it with Crabtree & Evelyn's Cox's Orange Pippin

Apple room spray. Put on a favorite tape and do some sit-ups and legwork. "Make it burn," as Jane Fonda would say. Sing to your favorite music. Enjoy the freedom of being in your own world. Follow with a delicious bubble bath of Crabtree & Evelyn's birch foaming bath gel and feel you've been on a vigorous walk in the woods. Go to bed for a ten-minute rest, wrapped in a huge terry-cloth robe. Treat yourself to reading *W* or *HG*. Experiment and hone your skills by pampering yourself. Why be out of sorts when you have options? Don't compromise and drink your morning coffee in any old mug—use a pretty decorative colored cup and saucer. Remind yourself you are serving coffee to someone you love and want to please! We all have little things that make our moments better; it is essential that we use them for ourselves as well as for others. Eliminate the expression "everyday" from your vocabulary. Don't have everyday dishes or everyday nightclothes. Each selection should celebrate the specialness of the moment. No moment upstages *the* moment. No one else is more important than you are.

When we're in the habit of doing everything graciously for ourselves, it becomes automatic that we do the same when we're in the company of others. Learn the discipline and skill of gracious living in the smallest details of your private daily life because it is these small humble ways that we do things that add up to our style, manner, and personality. Try to be the same person when you are alone as when you are with others. Don't let down—you'd only be letting yourself down. Smile. Listen to your silent voice. Think good thoughts. Look your best. Be charming. Be sensuous. Wear perfume when you're alone reading. Light the lights. Pleasure yourself. Be stimulating company.

We would be putting on airs if we did things for others that are not naturally what we do for ourselves. What we expect of others is understood only when we expect it of ourselves. We have hundreds of choices to make each day more lovely for ourselves and for others. When we make wise choices it moves us closer to a life of grace and fulfillment.

TAKING
TIME TO
APPRECIATE

Spread light.

Treasure your private time when you are free to appreciate the beauty around you. Open up all your senses. Be aware of the smells, the textures, and the noises of a quiet time. This will increase your hope and faith in life. Learn ways to inspire yourself by self-encouragement. Savor an achievement, past or present. Boost your spirits by remembering your many recent accomplishments. Do simple, satisfying tasks like sharpening pencils or straightening out the clutter on your desk. Absorb the joy and contentment you feel as you listen to some favorite music. Listen to Tchaikovsky, Bach, or Brahms. Make yourself a drink of fresh grapefruit juice mixed in a blender with ice until it is thick. Pour it into a hand-blown glass and sip it from a straw. Sit in a special spot near a window and read a book by a favorite writer—Chekhov, Johnson, Durrell, or Austen. I often reread specific passages and chapters when I'm seeking inspiration.

Never live without flowers—you need them to nurture your soul. I have a miniature yellow rose plant in a terra-cotta pot in the bathroom purchased at the New York Botanical Garden gift shop for four dollars and it has lots of tiny buds that are opening up. A friend was starved for flowers in her apartment and canceled her plans to take a four-day trip so she could buy flowering plants with the money instead. Her mood improved immediately. Hope is biologically and physically good for you. Hope increases when we are surrounded by natural beauty. Even if the city we live in is crowded and gray, we can choose to counterbalance it with the beauty and color of flowers. I have made it an absolute way of life always to have flowers in the rooms where I spend time alone and the places I share with others.

Develop the discipline of reading good literature daily. You must feed your mind with the best you can read because you will be influenced by what you select. Be stimulating to yourself as well as to those around you by reading and appreciating the classics. This way you will always be in good company. Last summer my husband Peter and I reread Edith Hamilton's *The Greek Way*. It tells about the purity, artistry, and balance of the Periclean Age which lasted only two hundred years. Afterward Greek life and outlook darkened and one can see in Hamilton's examples how this came about. This book led us to read more Sophocles, Aristotle, and Plato. I was searching for clues to help me better understand human beings' potential greatness, and the Greeks, in clear deep thinking, help to do just that.

I reread Henry Thoreau's *Walden* and was refreshed by the richness of simplicity and the wonder of being alone away from the madding crowd. Another great thinker, Lin Yutang, in his book *The Importance of Living* modestly identifies the true, lasting values so often obscured by the artificiality and tinsel of today. Edith Wharton's *Age of Innocence* eloquently illustrates society's manners and attitudes under the impact of economic and social change. I recommend reading Rollo May. Begin with his *Love and Will* which is an extraordinary, important book about sexuality, civilization, and contemporary morality. *Freedom and Destiny* is concerned with personal freedom. *The Courage to Create* reminds us that all creative acts are acts of courage because we are forming a new vision. *Psychology and the Human Dilemma* enlarges our outlook as we face loss of personal identity in the contemporary world. *My Quest for Beauty* is a joyful book which shows how our psychological well-being comes from the act of creating; this is illustrated with his own drawings and watercolors.

I think of this book as a storehouse of ideas—full of hundreds of ways each of us can reach toward greater self-awareness, appreciation of beauty, and love of others. When we find the process of our own lives a beautiful, exciting journey, we will automatically encourage, strengthen, and inspire other kindred souls. It is natural to give generously what you have personally discovered.

When people take short cuts, it robs them of the richness of life. Develop the habit of doing things beautifully out of the joy of making an effort for your own satisfaction. If you're enjoying yourself there is no such thing as being overly fussy. I tie colorful

The extra effort always makes the difference.

ribbons around things for the fun of it, knowing that an elastic band or tape won't give me the same pleasure. I use pretty ribbons as bookmarks. I have a set of sharp colored pencils on my desk in a glass so I can doodle with pretty colors and jot down a note in color instead of the usual gray lead.

Take action. Make an effort. If you find yourself in a rut, pay attention to the tiniest details of what you do. Remind yourself that everything you do, think, and dream matters. For example, when you're alone set an attractive table for dinner. Use your favorite china dinner plate and your best silver flatware. Make the effort to polish your knife, fork, and spoon so they sparkle. Dignify yourself in the smallest details. Use a big, ironed white cloth napkin. Take a few moments to arrange an attractive setting. When you pick up some fresh watercress at the store, buy a pretty rose or a bunch of daffodils on your way home. If you don't have access to fresh flowers, put some parsley in a vase or create a still life using fruit you brought out from the refrigerator. Natural beauty will keep you company at dinner. Don't forget to play some music, possibly the sound track from *Mission* or *Chariots of Fire*.

We tend to live up to our expectations of ourselves. Bathe and change your clothes for dinner. Wear a colorful blouse or shirt and slacks. Put on some cologne and smile in the mirror. Light a scented candle. You can enjoy a beautiful time alone in which you communicate your joys and concerns if you care enough to set an attractive stage and create a memorable ritual. You would do these things if a friend were to join you. Lift your spirits by doing these things for yourself. This allows solitude to be a celebration.

One night I found myself alone for dinner and I was feeling a bit edgy and sorry for myself. Peter, my husband, was away and my daughter Brooke had meant to come home but her plans changed. And I had so much work to do I couldn't sort out where to begin. My solution to almost everything is a long hot soak in the bathtub. Once relaxed, I realized how lucky I was to have this gift of time to catch up on my work. So I began with a pleasant dinner alone, rinsed my dishes, went into my home office off the kitchen, which I've painted a rich hunter green and refer to as my "green room," and got to work—rejoicing in the time alone so I could catch up. The point is that things become clarified once we nurture ourselves. Often what we need to get back on track is a bite of food in a pretty setting surrounded by things we love and a few minutes alone.

Another favorite thing for me to do when I'm home alone is to divide my time in two. The first block of time I use to work on the apartment. When I'm alone I can buzz around at a cheerful clip, polishing a table surface or a brass picture frame or rearranging objects on a table. I always have projects that require extra time, so I have a running list of things to do and I check them off as I accomplish them. The second half of my time is spent working on myself—I love to read, curled up in a comfortable chair in the living room with my feet up and listening to music. I make it a regular habit when I'm alone to use all the spaces where I live. So often the living room has other people in it that I like to treat myself to a private moment there. I feel my family's personality all around me and being alone intensifies my appreciation of them as I calmly feel their presence.

Everyone who knows me, no matter how casually, knows about my friendship with my mentor, Mrs. Eleanor Brown, founder and for many years head of the design firm McMillen Inc. and considered by many to be the doyenne of interior design in America. Now in the final stages of her life, two years shy of her one-hundredth birthday, she is in transition between life and death—and dying has now taken the upper hand. For over twelve years I have been preparing myself emotionally for her death, for what it will be like without her example, without her presence. As she lay in bed resting, I felt sadness at losing a friend. Rationally I realize it is time, but that doesn't diminish the pain of the final loss of an admired friend.

BEING
SELECTIVE

I can no longer ask for advice because Eleanor is too weak to find a meaningful answer for me. Her condition will not improve; no miracle will move the clock back thirty years. Eleanor Brown has been my friend for over half my life. Because she is over half a century older than I am, she has shown me, through her example, a grace, an appreciation of beauty, an honesty, that represent all the best qualities of civility and manners from an earlier generation. She set a standard that allowed me to see the world through Henry James's view. Life was authentic, artistic, and aesthetic. She is a living person through whom I can witness the grace of an earlier age. I have spent over twenty-five years looking up to Eleanor and trying to emulate her. This great lady has been there for me through all the ups and downs of my adult life, consistently showing genuine support and interest in my family, my career, my happiness.

We remember moments.

When my children were young and they'd put a milk carton on the kitchen table I'd inquire, "What would Mrs. Brown think?" The milk would then be poured into a pretty pitcher. They knew it was nicer but it also required an extra step. Whatever I find myself doing I wonder, "How would Eleanor solve this problem? What direction would Eleanor take? Wouldn't Eleanor love this white flower arrangement?" And when I get discouraged I question why I can't live the way she did—she seemed to have it all. But that's just the point: Eleanor Brown lived so beautifully because she did not have or do it all. She was very selective, and the things she chose to have and do were of a high standard of excellence. Eleanor disapproved of clutter. She never stretched herself too thin. There is only so much time, and living beautifully takes time and a great deal of self-restraint. She told all the decorators who worked for her that we had to be in training to live, feel well, and do a good job. She understood that we couldn't run around all day and stay out all night because decorating requires a great deal of energy.

Eleanor never rushed. The process was key to her. She savored each act whether it was rearranging furniture or sipping tea, and she did everything deliberately so nothing was vulgar or crass. She liked life to have an air of elegance and every single thing she said, thought, or did led toward that as a lifetime goal. Elegance, simplicity, and beauty.

When Mrs. Brown was in her early eighties I had been working for her design firm for many years. We went on a business trip to St. Louis together—she was born in St. Louis in 1890. We flew out to work on the interior design for the St. Louis Country Club. I was quite pregnant with my daughter Alexandra, and slightly uncomfortable from being squeezed into the small seat on the plane. My ankles were swollen and I had a stomachache. My baby was kicking quite vigorously.

DON'T
WORRY

We discussed how I'd manage to continue to work and also take care of my baby. With an air of complete confidence Mrs. Brown calmly stated, "Don't worry. We'll work it out." And that's exactly what we did. I didn't know how I'd manage, I just knew not to worry, she was behind me. Before the plane touched down, the conversation ended with our sharing our views about the self-fulfillment and gratification of making a contribution and being in a position to help people improve their lives. I'd had a taste of it and craved more, whereas she had spent her life in service to others and knew no other life. She told me how satisfying it was for her to spend a lifetime doing essentially what she loved to do and to be useful.

Eleanor Brown taught almost entirely through example. She had a husband and a son but still made herself available to those in her firm and we learned based on the ancient system of apprenticeship. We watched her and she watched us, and the values we learned have had a lasting effect on our lives and approach to solving problems. We came to understand that every room needs a touch of yellow, that all attractive rooms need a lot of wood surfaces, that when you repeat shapes you gain harmony. Eleanor taught through her actions.

ON YOUR OWN TERMS

She never sacrificed her own integrity as she quietly helped her clients. No one ever pushed Mrs. Brown around. When the late Charles Revson aggressively demanded a resolution to the scheme of his ballroom, Eleanor paused and told him firmly, "Mr. Revson, I have no answers today. I haven't dreamed on it yet." Her interests and talents were her vehicle to serve, and yet she did everything on her own terms.

As if out of the blue, one day in a taxi on our way to see a client she quietly but resolutely stated her belief, "I will *die* when my usefulness is up." Mrs. Brown is fortunate to have lived a long, useful life, a life that has so many lessons to teach, so much wisdom to impart. The first and greatest bit of wisdom was to think of life's big picture. The big picture was all-important. She always felt there would be time for everything important—do everything with a sense of excellence and things will work out. That was always the criterion.

Mrs. Brown knew how to remain healthy and vigorous by pacing herself. As a result of her wisdom, she outlasted all her peers and friends, remaining productive and in demand for decades after they faded away. Her fierce discipline provided tremendous options because it made her energetic beyond her years. I remember going to her apartment for small dinner parties where she would offer everyone a martini. If there were no takers she would gracefully walk over to a Louis XVI demi-lune table and prepare a martini straight up mixed in a small chilled silver shaker. She enjoyed this ritual and I never saw her have a second one. This great lady never overdid. She didn't like it when others did either.

She knew about the long haul. Her firm had strict hours and you had to leave by 5:30 P.M. or you were locked inside the townhouse. One evening I got carried away and, being on the top floor, wasn't aware that anyone else had left. I barreled down the stairs and triggered the alarms! Holmes Protection agency had to come get me. She was not amused. Working late was never rewarded.

"Enough is abundance to the wise."
—EURIPIDES

There was no overtime. Overdoing was a sign of disorganization to her. She wanted us to keep a steady pace, as had proven successful for her over many productive, rewarding years.

When she was in her mid-eighties the firm acquired a car and driver (in theory so she could move around more easily). Wrong. The young assistant decorators used the car because Eleanor preferred to walk. She left a little early so she could window-shop and scout for objects for clients. We all feel it was her love of walking, along with her use of the stairs of her duplex apartment and the five-story townhouse, that had a great deal to do with her stamina and good health. With her knowledge of life's greatest subtleties, she was amazingly resilient, changing her life as circumstances changed, never becoming a victim of an out-of-date idea or style.

Because she was my mentor I observed more than just her views on design, form, perspective, and color. I was able to have a close look at the person behind this great success and reputation. In 1922 Mrs. Brown's father had lent her $13,000 to start her company on the condition that she wouldn't take on any partners. She agreed and never betrayed her father's wishes. This pact with her father gave her fierce independence. I would like to be able to feel that sense of freedom at the end of my lifetime. She was free to pick and choose and did so wisely. Eleanor Brown surrounded herself with talented people who could help her to run her firm. "Success" was her favorite word and she thrived on its energy. Remember the social climate this lady tackled professionally. She even went to business school so she could know how to run her business more effectively.

A ROLE MODEL

In my private time I often wonder about how Mrs. Brown and I ever got together in the first place. Long before we met we had the mutual interest of design and art that led me to go work for her great firm. Yet it was much more than that for me. She represented something far more important than I had any idea of at the time. I needed her as a nurturing older role model as well as an elegant grande dame boss. I've grown to believe she enjoyed me as a young female image of a daughter she never had, or as a granddaughter she could influence by her interests. Eleanor's son, Louis, became an architect. Had she been born a male I'm sure she too would have been an architect.

Call it luck and timing, we loved doing the same things: going to art galleries, Saturday furniture auctions, art museums, the ballet, concerts; and eating good food, both at home and at restaurants. She shared my passion for eating out in restaurants—when I was pregnant we went to a health food restaurant and ate soybean salad. The firm's hangout was P. J. Clarke's pub, a hamburger joint, and we also went to good restaurants where she would test their lit- tleneck clams on a bed of ice and in the spring, asparagus vinaigrette. On Sunday mornings we'd go to hear a good sermon; on weekdays we'd walk to our next appointment with an eye to Madison Avenue window shopping; we'd go to galleries, antique shops; we'd ap- preciate architecture, shop for decorative objects—we shared so many things. I loved seeing her in her cutting garden in Southamp- ton coming into the house and arranging little bouquets for all the awaiting tabletops.

Mrs. Brown taught me that the more order, form, and harmony we bring to what we do, the better are the results. She taught me the importance of paying close personal attention to everything. Throughout the working day she would walk into an office and inquire, "Any problems?" Just knowing she personally would over- see everything stretched us to greater efforts.

In the process of writing this book, vivid images of Mrs. Brown constantly come to my mind. Things she's said—"Symmetry creates order," or, "One has to keep weekly expenses in line in order to have money to live." Because of my decorating work I was exposed to great wealth at a young age and she gently showed, by example, how each of us has to be true to ourselves financially. I also learned from Mrs. Brown that there is no such thing as a nine-to-five career. She kept those strict office hours so the rest of her waking time could be spent feeding her aesthetic interests. The ballet, theater, concerts, lectures, art openings, and fashion shows were all a big part of the picture. When she was interviewed by *House & Garden* at ninety-five years of age, she was asked how she separated her work from her social life. After a pause she answered, "I never had to. It all seemed to fit together somehow."

Albert Einstein's famous line "The most beautiful thing we can experience is the mysterious" reminds us that in science there will always be mysterious things we can't explain. Mrs. Brown made me more ready to open up to mystery. Gerald G. May, a psychiatrist with a private practice in Columbia, Maryland, discusses willingness and willfulness in his wise book *Will and Spirit*. He believes that we can control our lives to a great extent through our willfulness, but that we must also allow for a "willingness" to take place, in which we let go and let some mystery take over. He suggests we can "make friends" with mystery by waking up to whatever is really happening at each moment. May suggests that we notice, look around, and take a deep breath as we live in the present moment, and that we be willing to be who we are.

There are too many coincidental happenings that we can't explain, that seem magical when they happen. For instance, my friendship with Mrs. Brown happened by chance. I went to a lecture she was giving and I just knew I had to work for her. Three of my grandparents had died when I was seven and I needed Mrs. Brown in my life. It is perfectly possible that I would have had a lesser need for her presence if I had been able to love and experience my own grandparents. I had a void in my life and was receptive to having it filled in a new way. She provided what was missing for me.

These special moments can happen at any time. After struggling with a problem and feeling quite desperate, you may stumble across a passage in a book that leads you to a breakthrough—suddenly

WILL AND
SPIRIT

you have vision and clarity of thought. Or you may take an airplane and sit next to an "old soul," someone you feel you've known for centuries. Or you may have felt a little blue, and just at a moment of discouragement someone you adore telephones to say they are thinking of you.

A life well lived will embrace mysterious spiritual aspects. My aim is to inspire you to be more alert to all the opportunities available to you as you get to know yourself better. Once you know what you want, you automatically become connected with like-spirited people. Learn to recognize the presence of the mysterious in your daily life and trust your intuition. Feel the positive gifts and goodness in your life. Francis Bacon understood "a wise man will make more opportunities than he finds."

NURTURING A FRIENDSHIP WITH YOURSELF

Take time out.

The best way to have a friend is to be a friend. When I nurture a friendship with myself I am more receptive to reaching out in love to others. Eleanor Roosevelt advised us, "Friendship with oneself is all-important because without it one cannot be friends with anyone else in the world."

It is a shocking realization that we can't give what we don't have! As a result, I try to listen to warning signals of my own mental fatigue and take some sort of therapeutic action. Our mood obviously fluctuates with our energy level. A few weeks ago I was feeling tense and overly pressured and I'd temporarily lost my passion. So I rearranged my schedule in order to go down to the Federal Court House with my husband Peter, who is a lawyer, to watch F. Lee Bailey cross-examine the principal complainant for the prosecution in a criminal case. After three hours of the intensity of courtroom drama, I was raring to go again. My mind was clear and I was ready to tackle the work I love, but first I needed to nurture myself. Peter and I had a leisurely lunch at a newly opened French restaurant near the courthouse. That lunch and F. Lee Bailey's passion for his case helped me to get my energy back. Have you ever been exhausted and felt you could hardly lift a finger? Suddenly the telephone rings and you hear good news and you jump with joy, full of energy. More energy than we may realize is available to us if we just learn to tap into it.

The great dancer Fred Astaire made his feet perform miracles; he apparently knew how to flow and move with the music naturally. Yet in fact he worked extremely hard at his dancing, practicing right up until he went on stage—he did this all through his career. He had a personal commitment to dance, dance, dance, and to get better with each step. The result was that he made dancing look easy. Until *A Chorus Line* we hadn't seen people rehearsing their steps backstage.

TIME
TO HONE
YOUR SKILLS

Once we discover what we most want to do, then we need time to practice and perfect our skills so we can feel the exhilaration of excellence. Just tonight an actress friend declined having supper with me because she is rehearsing her lines for a morning taping of a new television series. Discipline. Focus. Timing. When we meet, it will be right for both of us.

Another friend, Melissa, plays the piano so beautifully that I melt when I sit back and listen to her. Over lunch we discussed her music. "I'm one of four children, and my mother and father let the children have piano lessons only if we practiced regularly. There were lots of instruments around the house. We all sang a great deal. When people tell me they love my piano playing, I thank them. As for the few who really want to listen, I tell them it's hard work. I've played every day, never skipping a day, for twenty-five years. Anyone could be pretty good with all that practice!" Loving what you do is essential because you will spend your life developing your skills.

Think of your life as a work in process. You know how often your mood changes, your energy lags, your enthusiasm comes and goes; you know your negative and positive thoughts, your smiling moments and your times of gloom and anguish. Pay attention to the signals as you go through your day. Are you more optimistic in the morning? If so, you should give yourself nurturing time in the morning so you can have your freshest, most "up" time to do your creative work. Make a few minor changes as you go through your day that will renew your optimism and give you a positive outlook. Make this your highest priority. Experiment. The possibilities for refreshment and discovery are endless. Make an "I wish" list and then take action so your wishes come true. Take voice lessons. Dance classes. Buy some watercolors and spend some time painting pictures of your garden flowers this summer. Learn to play the piano. Take a course on decorative painted finishes.

What can you do right this minute to feel good? I always feel wonderful after I wash my hair. Write a love poem or letter. Clean out a drawer and put a pretty sheet of marbleized paper in as a drawer liner. Wrap a gift for a friend in hand-sponged paper you made yourself. Do something that will put a smile on your face. Optimism leads to happiness and enthusiasm, which is all shared.

| TEN PERCENT FOR YOU | Most of us are awake an average of sixteen hours each day, or 960 minutes. Each week we can literally do hundreds of little things to fuel our own engines. If we spend as little as 10 percent of our time nurturing ourselves it will only add up to a little over eleven hours a week—not much more than an hour a day. If you spend 10 percent of your awake time nurturing the spirit in you, you are an honor student. If you can keep your high average over a long period of time, you merit an award. Make it a priority to exercise your mind by taking a course in creative writing or art history in the evenings. Share your excitement about Renaissance art with others. Write a short story or an article, and also share that. Take time to have your hair cut and styled because when you feel |

good about yourself and look attractive, that feeling is shared. Everyone around you receives the richness of your daily ituals of self-nurturing, the fullness of what you do when you are alone.

How can you be encouraged to keep up with your eleven hours plus a week in which you do something for yourself that you really enjoy? It doesn't matter what you choose as long as you fill up your own well so you have some refreshment and fresh insights to share with others. Whether you read, meditate, study, paint, garden, sculpt, swim, write, bake, play tennis, go to a museum, ride a horse, sew, stencil, buy something at auction, or rearrange your closet, it should be a matter of passionate concern. Do these self-nurturing things with intensity and abandon. This free time when you can let loose and have a love affair with life is the very spark that makes you the person others want to be around. *Do not feel guilty.* Ten percent of your time for you leaves ninety percent for others. Take all ten percent each week. Put in your hour plus a day. Take one day at a time. Plan your week carefully and enjoy the anticipation of each deliberate act. You set your schedule. You are not indispensable. The plans you make for yourself are as important as anything that could keep you from your plan. Keep track. If you miss a day, make it up to yourself. Experiment in ways your self-nurturing time can best benefit you. One week, plan two or three hours in one day and skip a day. Another week, take time each day and see what suits you best. We tend to have a love-hate relationship with the very disciplines that keep us healthy and our lives in balance. Take stock. If you take ninety minutes and feel you need more, rearrange your schedule so you can add more self-nurturing time.

Self-caring is being responsible and not allowing any excuses. Make this pattern a way of life. Some people, because of their circumstances, can find 20 percent of their awake time to pursue private interests that don't directly or immediately relate to others. Remember that all the time spent nourishing yourself will enrich and strengthen your time and your relationships with others. Don't wait for permission: this is the secret to great human happiness and once you start, you will set yourself on a path that will lead to places of great beauty and happiness.

In academic life, no student spends all of his or her time studying. Peter and I have two daughters in college and think they have a generous amount of time off. We, too, can't work all the time; we need a break. Because we don't have bells ringing, recesses, and vacations after tests and exams, we tend to let tension build up. Yet we need to regenerate ourselves and it's up to us to give ourselves the breaks we need. Others can't do this for us. We have to learn to feel comfortable being unavailable. Women often get caught in the trap of feeling indispensable. We tend to be mother hen and want to oversee and do everything. We don't have it all—rather, we *do* it all. We worry about why we aren't perfect, and when our unrealistic expectations are not met we feel let down, drained, discouraged.

I've discovered it isn't healthy to be "there" all the time—not for a spouse, not for a child, not for a parent, not for a job, and not for a friend. Not for anyone. We have to concentrate more on being here for *ourselves*, in a regular way. We can't guarantee we'll always be available to others but we can control our availability to ourselves. All we can do for others is try our best.

I understand I can't be a savior to others. It's a big enough task to save myself. I believe the notion of perfection is dangerous to our well-being and keeps us from living to our fullest potential with others. We are all human. Strive, persist—and then relax. Live with the knowledge that you have done your best. Learn the art of compromise so that all your energy remains positive. Expect some problems and they won't seem so disappointing when they come. Lower your expectations so that you are happier with the reality of the moment at hand. Unrealistic expectations leave you forever disappointed.

A highly successful woman, pregnant with her first child, in-

Experience teaches
more than logic.

quired, "How did you work so hard, raise children, and still find the time and energy to entertain?" I laughed. I found Jean's question amusing. I love my work, and I also love my friends. I only have two children: they're now away at college. I know my limitations of time, money, and energy and I've learned from Mrs. Brown to keep things simple. I serve simple food at my parties. How can you go wrong with fresh ingredients? I vividly remember having a dinner party for our favorite artist, Roger Mŭhl, in 1969. He and his wife Line were in New York from Paris for an exhibition and everything was perfect except one thing. I'd forgotten to breast-feed Brooke and just as our guests piled in the door, Brooke wailed in need! I disappeared for forty-five minutes and the party seemed to manage quite well without me. I learned an important lesson that night. It's okay to be human.

Last winter I cooked for our friend Roger Vergé, the chef from Moulin de Mougins in France. He was in the United States promoting his new book *Entertaining in the French Style*, and we had a party for him. Friends who are accomplished amateur cooks confessed they'd be afraid to cook for a three-star chef. I'm rarely afraid because I'm having so much fun and I keep everything simple. We had a veal roast and fresh steamed vegetables. Vergé seemed to enjoy eating our food. He knows I'm no famous chef. There is so much more to entertaining than just the food. We all shared toasts and laughs and the food was really far less important than the pleasure of being together. Entertaining makes you feel good as you make others happy. When you really want someone to be at your dinner table, it creates a warm, friendly atmosphere.

When you eliminate the idea of perfection, nothing can hold you back. You lose your fear. Perfectionists don't enjoy the real world because they're too critical. They put themselves down and everyone else, too. Perfection is the death of spontaneity, originality, and good fun. People who take risks, who are creative and love to experiment and improvise, who make the best of what they have, tend to have more fun day to day.

TIME OFF   Think of your nurturing time as recess. Teachers have a snack. Soldiers marching get ten-minute breaks every hour so they can march farther. Union workers have coffee breaks. Ministers take time out to meditate, and go on retreats for renewal. You and I need a few regular breaks, too. Take them. Disappear and have a nap or a massage or a walk alone. Learn to feel comfortable with yourself when you escape. Alone, you find your center and feel better about not only yourself but everything else. You need time to think things through and listen to your own voice, because everyone else has something else in mind for you. You can't react to others' ideas of who and what you are; you have to be authentically you.

Every once in a while, be a slob. That may sound funny, but you can live a beautiful life and occasionally be a slob. You can also have a sloppy house from time to time. Because I'm a decorator, people constantly apologize to me for the condition of their homes. "I'm sorry the windows are dirty. I'm sorry there are no flowers in the house. I'm sorry the bed isn't made." I enjoy it when things are a little messed up because it means there has been some real living going on. So what if, one day a week, you don't have the cleanest house on the block? We can't wait until every last dust ball has been eliminated before we stop to relax.

My friend Lindsay Findlay runs an art gallery and works six days a week. It wears her out. Every once in a while she has an "Alexandra Day." You stay in bed as long as you like, you stay in your nightclothes, you read, relax, and let the world pass you by for a day or half a day. I usually do this Saturday mornings. It's a great luxury to take half a day off. If you wait until you're sick you won't be able to really appreciate the luxury of your free time. It's best to take time off as you go along and avoid getting sick from being run-down.

People tend to live in all-or-nothing zones. They have to have everything just so or they collapse. Things tend to swing from

Staying in bed when you aren't ill is a treat.

black to white, fat to thin, leaving too little tolerance for the real personality. Only you and I know how it really feels to push too hard and rarely enjoy a little moment's peace. The tennis player Arthur Ashe says: "You've got to be intense when it counts. If you try to be intense twenty-four hours a day, you're not going to last very long."

Jane Brody wrote an article in the *New York Times* on dieting, pointing out that "a minor lapse needn't be seen as a major fall from grace." Brody said, "Experts on behavior have identified what is probably the most potent factor undermining successful weight control: self-defeating attitudes. It all boils down to unrealistic expectations."

Dr. Kelly D. Bromwell, a psychologist at the University of Pennsylvania, calls this all-or-nothing attitude "Light-bulb think-ing—you're either on the diet or off it. This dichotomous thinking . . . can doom the dieter to failure. . . . One day's indiscretion should not ruin any diet." The trick is to bounce back. Learn to moderate yourself as you go along.

Instead of saying you don't have time to exercise, start. Nibble away at it. Put on some sneakers or ballet slippers with the elastic strap and run around your apartment or house tidying up. It's exercise with a purpose! Tackle a wedge, a piece. Even if you can't manage a whole hour of Jane Fonda, do fifteen minutes. Your body will appreciate anything good you do for it. Jump rope or ride an exercise bike while watching the news. Don't be rigid and doom yourself to failure because you are busy. Chances are the busier you are the more you'll enjoy yourself—you have to learn to use the slices of the day to do a little of this and that. It all adds up. The headmistress of a top girls' school in New York squeezes her fanny muscles—an exercise she learned in her exercise class—while waiting for elevators or for a meeting to start. The exercise increases circulation and keeps your back strong. Wasting time is agoniz-ing, but when you "squeeze, squeeze, squeeze" you are using your time well.

Virginia Woolf once commented, "It is far harder to kill a

phantom than a reality." Living a perfect life is a myth. Feeling good about yourself, enjoying yourself as you appreciate all the good and positive influences around you, is a wonderful way to live.

TAKE ACTION   Regularly clean out your emotional closet. Take stock of your feelings. Express your gladness in tangible ways. Clap your hands. Skip to the kitchen. Smile. Rearrange the sagging flowers, polish a piece of silver. Sing. Iron some wrinkled napkins. Straighten out your linen closet. First, line the shelves with scented, flowered shelf paper and then trim the shelf with colorful striped grosgrain ribbon, glued on with Elmer's glue. Stretch your arms and sigh "ah." Do little things that reward you so you bounce up with a positive frame of mind. I have a friend in Birmingham, Alabama, whose motto is "think up." Every time she faces a problem or a slump—a bad mood—she "thinks up" and immediately does something to pamper herself. File your nails, rub some Chanel No. 5 body cream on your hands, arms, and elbows; rinse out your pantyhose in some almond soap; or write an art postcard to a friend. Say a prayer. Hum a hymn. Browse through a favorite art book. Wax your desk.

Often when we take these minibreaks we see what seems to be bogging us down. What have you been putting off doing that needs to be done? It can be as simple as making a "to do" list and then numbering the list in order of priority. I think best on paper. Whenever I clarify on paper what is dragging me down, I'm able to spring into action. Doing something—whatever it is—releases our trapped energy. Never let your energy get blocked. You gain energy by exerting energy, so whenever you feel blue do something active. Energetic people have fun.

Dr. Wayne Dyer, author of many self-help books, points out that since we only have a certain number of minutes on earth, why waste a chunk of them in a state of anxiety? Your life is worth more than that.

Ask yourself what you have been putting off that makes you feel guilty. Ask yourself why. Possibly you don't have your heart in the task in the first place. Usually when we drag our heels and procrastinate we aren't fully engaged. Do you have an article due? Is it an article you want to write? Can you thrive under the pressure of your deadline or are you miserable? Are you behind in your correspondence? With your office paperwork? Are you behind answering telephone calls? Are your brass and silver tarnished, your mirrors cloudy, and your furniture unpolished? These things can eat away at you. Get them done and put them behind you. Your passport needs renewing. Your car doors don't lock and the car needs to go in for repair. You have to go to the dentist because you have an aching tooth. Don't put things off. In light of the importance of life, this stuff is trivia. Do it now, not later. Get it behind you. Don't *you* be behind. Make a plan and set a realistic schedule for yourself so that you are set free.

Write these things down. Schedule time to tackle them, one at a time. Make a check mark after a task is completed. Get satisfaction from every job well done, no matter how humble, by checking it off when it's completed. Then reward yourself. Dream big dreams. If you want to study anthropology, don't feel you have to know the contents of the textbook before you enter the classroom. You don't need to master the whole subject in one gulp—you're there to learn, one class at a time. Be kind to yourself because you've taken care of all the clutter in your life that can bog you down and make you feel guilty.

Whenever I really need to pull myself together I reread some of Rilke's *Letters to a Young Poet*. These letters give me a glimpse of what goes on behind the scenes in other people's lives and show me how much beauty is everywhere if I am "poet enough to call forth its riches." Rilke's poetry is very accessible and lovely. We must remind ourselves that each day we make fresh beginnings.

Maybe you're the mother of a young schoolchild and something aches inside you, making you feel guilty you're not home as a full-time mother. The truth is, you're probably more able to be reached by the school authorities in an emergency when you're at an office than you would be if you didn't work, when you might be out doing volunteer work or errands. And if you want to be a class mother or chaperone at a school event you probably are organized enough to manage that—for if it's what you want to do, you can find a way.

Your mother may have been president of the garden club and you may live in the city and not even have a garden. Maybe you're the first woman in your family to have a challenging career, breaking the traditional cycle, and you don't have a role model to follow. You may wonder why you don't live as well and as beautifully as your parents did, but I believe that you and I are living a full life and doing the best we can. It's all in your perspective. Remember just how different your life *is*—you shouldn't look at the way things were for your parents. Do the things you believe in and the things that make a difference. Choose wisely. When I feel out of synchronization, I always think of what Anaïs Nin once said, "The dream was always running ahead of me. To catch up, to live for a moment in unison with it, that was [is] the miracle."

So, take time out. Take time to think about your choices, and choose things you need to do and want to excel in. Meryl Streep has to make new rules every day as the mother of three young children, the wife of a sculptor, and a major film star. Guard your privacy so that you too are in a position to pursue the things you most believe in.

Do some soul searching. What areas of your life need improvement? Maybe you really need more exercise. You should take more time for reading. Or, analyze honestly that you need to lose weight. Don't ask a friend. If you're a pretty good dancer and, more important, you enjoy dancing, take dance classes and watch the pounds shed. Become thin again for yourself so that you're happy with your appearance. Will you ever have a perfect body? Probably not. To be fit and look and feel well, that's good enough. So dance a little, walk a little, climb up stairs, exercise a little, diet a little, eat and drink a little less.

If you are thinking of someone to whom you want to write, drop a line, don't wait to write a proper letter. One line on a postcard has great impact—certainly more than no letter at all. If you have never read Dickens, pick up a paperback edition of *Great Expectations* and read a few pages a day. Think of small steps you can handle.

Eleven hours a week—nurture yourself. Watch out for signs of the devil. American households watch an average of forty hours of television a week. Set strict limits. Television is passive. Give yourself regular and necessary nurturing time. If you're a full-time homemaker, do everything with a sense of grace and ease. Dignify your choices. Go pick mulberries, sketch in the field, go on nature walks, sit on the grass with a child and play. Tumble down a meadow. Press flower petals in a book. Play jacks. Checkers. Play in the autumn leaves. During a child's nap, sew or make things for the house or write prose. Call a friend and invite her to tea if you're in the mood for adult company. There is lots of time. Be creative with the time you have and do everything with flair and a sense of fantasy.

Whatever you decide to do, make it a wonderful experience. Make a list each morning of all the fun, happy things you intend to do that day. Before you go to sleep at night, check to see how you scored for that day. Having high hopes can be a self-fulfilling prophecy.

When you are at your best, you are your own best friend. You don't have to cut your hair off because short hair is easier and faster to take care of; maybe you really enjoy the private time you spend washing, blow-drying, and styling your gorgeous hair, to say nothing of the pleasure you get all day from having shiny long hair. If you need ten minutes a day to have lovely hair, give yourself this, if you decide it's satisfying to you. Or maybe you really get a kick out of having pretty hands and nails. The time and effort you spend caring for your nails is relaxing and soothes you. Maybe you enjoy caring for your feet. It doesn't really matter what you decide to focus on when you have this free time. All that matters is that you are doing these self-pampering things for your own contentment, never as some burden to complain about or something to brag about. Keep these pleasures to yourself.

If you'd rather spend your free time reading Cicero's book *On the Good Life*, go to it: I highly recommend it. If, however, you choose to paint your nails and one of your nails breaks, it is not worthy to discuss this with others.

"We all live in suspense," Mary McCarthy tells us. "From day, to day, from hour to hour, in other words, we are the hero of our own story." Guard your free time. It is better to be free and decide to do something on the spur of the moment than to be tied up and have no freedom to choose according to your mood. Do what the spirit moves you to do. Turn on a favorite record and dance alone. You'll feel better immediately. If you need a lift, go indulge yourself in a new shade of lipstick or a silk handkerchief for your jacket. Buy a new cologne. Browse in a favorite book or record store. Go to a thrift store and rummage around. Whenever we experience these innocent nonevents for ourselves we emerge refreshed. Often we just need a mini-escape.

Never tell anyone what your mini-escapes are. Everyone has to work things out backstage. But when the curtain opens you are energized; there is a current of energy you give off to others. Sparked by your private self-nurturing, you give your best to each moment.

If you're being true to yourself, that's enough. You really can't worry what others think or you'll never do anything original and never be authentic. Everything good in your life is motivated by self-knowledge. Come to grips with your individualism: There is no one like you anywhere. Any great artist creates from the heart, not from what will please others. That should be our goal as well.

When you discover lots of delightful things you can do for yourself that make you a happier, more secure person, you'll find you actually bring pleasure and delight to others too. Little things turn from mundane to pleasurable because of your attitude. Open your net to the vast possibilities. Don't be too hard on yourself even if you goof up a bit along the way.

Be brave and bold. Take risks. Trust yourself. Dwell on your successes and what you know makes you happy. Dare to become uncomfortable as you stretch yourself for a more vital, dynamic feeling inside. Develop a love of your whole life—what you do, whom you love, and where you live. "Avoiding danger is no safer in the long run than outright exposure," Helen Keller advised. "The fearful are caught as often as the bold." If you have powerful big fears to work through and are afraid, this might be a time you need extra self-nurturing and rest. You will have great moments of discovery, contentment, and grace once you allow yourself a minimum of eleven hours a week to nourish a friendship with yourself. Mark your calendar now to take yourself to lunch this week. Indulge yourself in a favorite dish and savor your own company.

If you find you lie awake at night worrying about something you weren't able to solve during the day, do what my friend Camille does. Just like changing the television channel, change your worry to a bedtime story in which you are the star. Reassure yourself that you are wonderful. You'll fall asleep thinking happy thoughts. Give yourself time; you are better able to help yourself than anyone else.

Slowly, burnish your own philosophy. "Unless each day can be looked back upon by an individual as one in which he has had some fun, some joy, some real satisfaction," said Dwight D. Eisenhower, "that day is a loss." We are not alone but connected, dependent on one another for the true and beautiful possibilities in life. Each of our lives can be witness to how we can remain civilized and open to one another, how we can move steadily toward our own goals and encourage those we love, believing that together we can make a difference. Together we can make more opportunities than we find. Joy is hidden in the least obvious places.

- Plant some herbs or potted flowers and watch them grow.
- Go on a morning meditation walk alone for a week and see if it can become a daily habit.

GRACE
NOTES

- Revive an old plant—give it a new pot and trim off the dead leaves. You will feel like a miracle worker.

- Think "up."

- Savor some personal accomplishment; go out to dinner with a friend and celebrate.

- Begin a "dream" file. Clip articles about exotic places, restaurants, beauty tips, and fashion and decorating ideas and look through it when you need a lift.

- "Be a friend to yourself, and others will." (Scottish proverb)

- Rub Tiger Balm on your lower back when you feel a bit tired; it gives you an instant lift.

- Collect beautiful flower-decorated blank greeting cards and always save one of each kind for yourself. Keep them in a basket with the colors peeking out for instant cheer.

- Before going to sleep, lie in bed and pick out one thing that you did well that day and congratulate yourself. You can build on that tomorrow.

- Sing along with your favorite singer. This is how Barbra Streisand learned to sing as a little girl.

- Write a list of what's right and wrong in your life; this is a great way to sort out your feelings.

- When you feel blue, sit down at your desk and write yourself a love letter.

- Go to a palm reader or have your tea leaves read.

- Guard your private time as your most treasured asset.

- Take a walk in the woods with a field guide; learn to identify different trees, animals, birds.

- Buy a small notebook. Glue on a pretty painting cut out from a magazine and begin your own quotation book. When you think of positive inspirational thoughts, write them down. "The glass is half full" can be your first entry. Try to jot down one or two each day.

- Weed out your Filofax. Buy new colorful pastel paper refills—plain or lined—for the fun of more color in your life.

- Take a course at a botanical garden, an art appreciation course at a museum, or a cooking course.

- Take aptitude tests to help define your natural abilities. You may be surprised at your hidden talents. Check in the yellow pages of the telephone book for career centers that offer these tests.

- Before you get out of bed in the morning, stretch your legs and arms, yawn, and then visualize an ideal day. Think about your vision throughout the day.

- Go back to your home town, the school you attended; it will bring back your childhood.

- Polish all your shoes and put in scented shoe trees.

- No time to read all those books on the bestseller list? Listen to a book on a headset on your way to work.

- Take a weekend trip by yourself. Do exactly what you want to do for two days. This will be a time of discovery and renewal.

- When you hear a good joke, tell it to someone right away so you won't forget the punch line. This will make you remember it so you can make lots of people laugh.

- Be adventurous—go to a movie by yourself.

- Line your drawers with scented flowered-paper drawer liners.

- Take a guided tour of a museum, then go home and read a book about your favorite artist.

- On a star-filled evening, go to an observatory.

- Buy a telescope. Contemplate the great unknown.

- Buy a book and get lost in a new topic.

- Laugh out loud.

- Read some vintage magazines found in a flea market: What was news back then; who was President? What did the ads show? What were people wearing? What were the popular sayings?

- Get out that camera that's been hanging in the closet; record the things around you and send the photos to a friend who's moved away, or save them for your children.

- Order a furniture kit and assemble the piece of furniture yourself. Your hands are more dexterous than you might imagine.

- Call an old friend with whom you've lost touch. Follow through with a note card. Mark your calendar to send another in a month.

- Try that recipe you clipped and still haven't made, and invite friends to sample your creation.

- Do solo sports: swim laps, do aerobics to music, run, ride your bicycle; now is the time to really think.

- Sign up for a yoga class.

- Sing in the shower.

- Clean out your clothes closet; get the satisfaction that comes from organization. Rearrange everything artistically so your eye is pleased. Spray your closet with your favorite room spray or buy cedar eggs or blocks.

- Rummage through your attic and treasure chests, or your old yearbooks—get lost in the memories.

- Reread your favorite book. Fill a notebook with your favorite lines and quotes.

- Get up early one day a week and treat yourself to a great breakfast out.

- Try getting up extra early and take a walk around the block; there *are* surprises in your neighborhood.

- Walk a different way to the station, or drive a different road; make even the most routine things different.

- Visit a farmer's market or roadside stand and delight in the sensual experience. Gather fresh vegetables and create a nourishing vegetable soup using a chicken-stock base.

- When you travel alone bring some of your mate's cologne with you to scent your pillow. It will make you close in spirit.

- Take advantage of the changing seasons; in the fall go apple picking. Make apple tarts. Make homemade applesauce. Bake apples with cinnamon and cloves.

- Meditate in the bathtub.

- Keep notepaper and a pen right next to your bed so you can drop a line to someone as you think of them.

- Start a collection. It can be anything that strikes your fancy. Read up on it and check the going prices in collector's field guides. You will love the challenge of expanding your little collection.

- Eat a meal in front of a mirror—alone—and carry on an interesting conversation with yourself.

- Volunteer at a hospital; giving a little bit of yourself is a remedy that even medicine can't top.

- Become active in your community, or a cause you believe in.

- Help your elderly neighbors; take an hour to visit and just chat; ask if they need anything when you go to the store.

- Look people squarely in the eye when talking with them.

- Stand up straight.

- Remember people's names. You have to first *know* a name to *remember* a name. When you hear it, repeat it and make an association with name and person.

- Make a list of the reading you want to do and make a schedule so there will be time to read.

- Arrive early for your appointments. It gives you a chance to compose yourself.

- Smile!

- Learn several new words each week and use them in your verbal and written expressions.

- Make a conscious effort to be positive. It shows great character and spirit.

- Structure silent time into your daily routine; it will give you additional energy.

- Make a monthly date to go to your local museum to see a few of your favorite paintings. Mark your date book. Go see some familiar pictures which become friends.

- Give yourself ten extra minutes to do something when you're under pressure; take your time and you will accomplish more.

- Each day make a list of things to do; you'll feel in control.

- Stop procrastinating.

- Don't forget to pamper yourself—go to a spa for the weekend. Can't afford it? Take a bubble bath, give yourself a facial, or go out and treat yourself to a manicure and a pedicure.

- Learn calligraphy.

- Count your blessings and don't stop until you have reached one hundred.

- Before going to sleep at night, pray for ten people you love.

- On days you know will be tough, wear your favorite outfit; you'll feel extra-confident.

- Challenge yourself to do the things you've always dreamed about: trekking in Nepal.

- Keep names of people you love who are having a tough time on the mirror of your dressing table to remind you of them—thoughts lead to action.

- It's helpful to keep a special prayer in your wallet or framed on your desk. We all need a spiritual lift now and then.

■ Examine and refurbish your luggage. It follows you around wherever you go and friends see it too.

■ Rehearse your toasts, introductions, and speeches in the bathroom mirror. Record them. Don't be shy.

■ Exercise and take two to three inches off your stomach and thighs. This does wonders for your self-confidence, and will give you energy and make you more outgoing.

YOUR
GRACE
NOTES

Part Two

LIVING

TOGETHER

The more personal harmony we feel the more we will be able to give in a loving relationship. All the elements necessary for a genuine, loving relationship with someone else are the same ingredients we need in order to fully love ourselves. Respect, confidence, good values, tolerance, open-mindedness, sincerity, benevolence—we share this inner contentment and self-love with someone. First, it has to be inside us. I must be sensuous and tender and intimate with myself before I can act that way with someone else. I must love myself privately with no thought of reward so I can love and help someone else without being paid back. Loving *is* the reward.

When love is not genuine it is disguised as self-sacrifice, and that ends up being calculating and demanding, where someone wants gratitude. Love never manipulates. If nurturing yourself is an act and must be learned, once mastered it deepens self-love. This self-love brings you independence and strength. Dependency on another person to make you function is immature and can interfere with genuine love.

When two people decide to live beautifully together they can complement each other, and each harmonious whole person can form a greater wholeness in partnership. Most of us live with some-

LIVING TOGETHER

". . . two solitudes protect and touch and greet each other."
—RAINER MARIA RILKE

one else. Living together with someone requires understanding their attitudes, expectations, and habits. Whether we are married couples, partners, or roommates, living together well is an art that requires paying attention to a great many details at one time and being able to do it all again the next day. We are challenged to be consistently at our best because when we aren't, we don't live well with others.

We have to learn to be as efficient as possible so things will run smoothly, and when they don't, be a good sport; right the wrongs and start all over again. The better things go today, the more chances for pleasure and harmony tomorrow.

I've discovered that, left to our own devices, we can get along quite well alone, day to day. If we feel lazy and don't make our bed, no one notices. If we don't empty the wastebasket, no one really cares. No one complains and no one explains.

Sharing ourselves with others, living together, we tend not to be bothered by our own eccentricities and laziness as much as we are upset by the habits of others. We can leave a messy sink, quite oblivious to our thoughtless act, but when we go to the kitchen and discover a mess someone else left, we have a different feeling. This is human nature at work—to react to others' acts and manners with more scrutiny than to our own. We tend not to observe ourselves as well as we see others for the simple reason that once we make ourselves aware, then we have to do something about it. Most of us have gone to the refrigerator, grabbed a leftover piece of chicken, eaten it Tom Jones style, reached for the carton of milk, had a gulp or two, rinsed our hands in the kitchen sink, and gone back to our book or television or to bed. We don't think twice. Yet, when we observe this, depending on how tired or hungry we are and how much stress we're under, we think, "No plate? No glass? No napkin? I'm living with a slob." We do these things but we'd rather live more graciously. We see the side in others that is the side we want to improve in ourselves.

The chicken snack could have been a lovely ritual if you had selected a pretty plate and a blue handblown glass for the milk. The napkin could be a huge blue-and-white checked kitchen dish

"Manners are the happy ways of doing things."
—*RALPH WALDO EMERSON*

towel you use as a lap napkin. When this is put on a tray, along with a little jar with some pickles and olives, salt, pepper, and French mustard, your nibbling chicken is turned into a pleasant moment.

Even better would be for the mate creating the lovely tray with the chicken to invite you to have some, too, it's hardly any extra effort, and then you would both have a special moment together, a bonus, a time when you can sit together and talk. So even the smallest act is an opportunity for sharing. If one of you has the desire for a bite of chicken, chances are the other will find that appealing when it is attractively served. Do this with decaffeinated espresso at an odd time, setting up an attractive tray, adding lemon rind and cinnamon stick as the stirrer. Try cheese and fruit as another unplanned moment to share.

When something is done nicely it creates a "moment of being" out of thin air and it is nice to share it as a gift with the one you live with.

We affect others by our habits and while it is normal to want to let down at home, not only do we have to be constantly considerate of the person or persons we live with, we should also continue to make the necessary extra effort to please ourselves.

In this chapter I want to speak about how we can discover new possibilities for a great deal of pleasure in sharing ourselves with someone else. When we have our home in harmony it is easier to have the other areas of our lives work out well. Home is our base, giving us the necessary roots and providing a place where we can create our own reality by the choices we make. None of us studied "home life" at college but there are ways of managing that free us to live with more grace and ease. This chapter focuses on fresh ideas to improve your home life.

We rejoice together.

When we marry we are in a state of becoming. Marriage is an adventure of the spirit, providing the opportunity to satisfy fun-

PARTNERS

Embrace the
unexpected.

damental yearnings and a need to belong. Marriage is also a contract and because it involves someone else, you can't be certain how you or your spouse are going to uphold the terms of the agreement. Together you work things out as you go along. An employer can put an employee on an initial three-month trial period; yet even though statistics indicate that 85 percent of wives and husbands marrying today have lived together beforehand, there is no way of knowing what marriage is really like until the knot is tied. "We understand so poorly the inner life of the people who are closest to us," observed the late bacteriologist and writer René Dubos. In his book *Beast or Angel* he stated, "Every organism, animal, as well as human, lives in a private world of its own to which no one has complete access."

With eyes half open we believe in the ancient myth that we have found our other half and are finally made whole. We can set out to sea and sail in good weather, together, forever. That is the myth, the promise, the hope and fantasy. How much of this is reality depends on our attitude, aspirations, chemistry, and good luck. When you marry, statistics say your chances are about 50-50 that your marriage will last.

It is easier to get into the boat on a glorious summer day than to bail out after a violent and threatening winter storm. Marriages, like sailing, have an enormous range of adventure and discovery; many things are in our control and an equal number beyond our control.

Marriage encompasses all the paradoxes: We have an awareness of our self and our uniqueness, yet we want to belong. We are individual, yet we want to be connected. All things are possible when we are motivated to transcend the necessities of everyday life into a foundation for joy through love. Robert Louis Stevenson reminds us: "To miss the joy is to miss all."

There are unknown questions when any two individuals unite. How well will we respond together to celebrations, holidays, financial success, bad luck, tragedy, loss, disappointment, and illness? How well will we cope when faced with failure, financial setbacks, or death? What capacity do we have together for keeping the household checkbook balanced? How well can we maintain an even and relatively cheerful disposition for possibly half a century? How well will we understand each other? How well will we listen? What effects will stress, fatigue, alcohol, and illness have on our manners and sensitivity over the years?

How well will we respond to aging? What kind of effort will each of us make to resist temptation when the devil knocks? How well will we balance family and work? What kind of parents will we be become? What values will we inculcate into the fiber of our children's character? How kind and tender will we be when things go wrong, how supportive in times of real crisis? Will we pay attention to the house as well as to the people in it? How much freedom will our partner allow us for our individual discoveries and unique aspirations? How much support will we give in helping our partner discover deeper potentials and richer satisfactions? These are some of the questions; your marriage will explore many of your answers.

Accept the unanswered questions that are a natural part of your new bond. And love the questions. Will we still feel attractive to each other thousands of days from now? Will we be perfectionists so that no one can live up to our expectations? How well will we cope when we let ourselves down? These questions may not occur to us as we sip rum punch on an island honeymoon gazing into a starry future. Think the best thoughts and take good care of everything in your control each day as it comes.

In ten years you'll have spent 3,650 days together. Live each day as if it is the first and last of your life together. Create images of the two of you together on a lovely sunny day on a deserted island. Think of the intimacy, the smiling, the listening, the laughter. Bring that home. And tomorrow, and tomorrow.

When two intelligent people, bound together in love, have the rest of the their lives to create a special, sacred, unique world for themselves, far greater than they could have without the added dimension of the other, it is worth every effort to explore how to

"The meeting of two personalities is like the contact of two chemical substances: if there is any reaction, both are transformed."
—CARL JUNG

make this relationship thrive. The rules have changed as women have gained more independence and control over their own lives and this causes adjustments in the way we manage the home. But the changes can be positive for both partners, and each couple will manage differently.

Set a goal that you want to live beautifully every day, enriching and expanding the other's vision, at the same time exploring your own individual talents and possibilities. The most important first step toward keeping your marriage vital, fresh, and loving is to live as lovers. Each partner treats the other with kindness, tenderness, and love. That is the secret. If this seems overly simple, it is the truth. As a residential interior designer I've worked all over the world and I've observed hundreds of marriages. The beautiful relationships among married couples are always carried out as though they were two young lovers, as though they were shipwrecked on a sunny deserted beach. Lovers do things together and share; they show a great deal of interest in their partner's special talents and passions. When both people pull together in this manner, the relationship thrives because each partner is giving and receiving an abundance of love.

Twenty-five years ago when I began my career as a professional interior designer I made my choice to be primarily a residential designer. I was warned that was not where the "big" money was—commercial work is more lucrative—but I knew where my heart was. Coming from a family of ministers, social workers, and artists, I jumped into a field which seemed a natural and I've never looked back. My work has brought me into the bedrooms, bathrooms, and kitchens of people all over the United States and I've also worked in Paris, Singapore, England, and Greece.

I have gained insights into the dynamics of relationships as I have worked on people's homes. I get to see the whole picture, the reality of a typical day in a couple's life. I have to know vivid details of how people interact in order to help them create a functional, attractive background for their lives. The information I receive is confidential—I know how they spend their money; I'm in their medicine cabinets, silver chests, linen closets, and dressing rooms. I know how many pairs of shoes they have and how many spices they use for cooking. I look inside bureau drawers and refrigerators and behind curtains. I go where couples live and my regular "house calls" allow me to be a fly on the wall. I become "family" and am intimately brought inside.

The happiest couples are the ones who both share a strong love of home. If both people are not equally concerned about the way their house or apartment functions, looks, and feels, it is usually a danger sign in the relationship. When a spouse is too busy to be in on the decisions it usually indicates he or she has tuned out and psychologically lives elsewhere. What greater use of our time can there be than to build a home with someone with whom we have made a commitment of love? When couples develop a mutual interest in art or antiques or gardening, they share more happiness and find more enrichment from their shared time at home.

One couple I know go to auctions on weekends as a regular hobby and they've not only learned a great deal about antiques, they've helped furnish their lovely big clapboard house in Litchfield, Connecticut. They have floor plans that guide them to hunt for furniture and objects that are the appropriate scale, and they enjoy the fun of sharing in the purchase of these important items for their home. Another couple spends their free time going to galleries, lofts, and art auctions, seeking young American artists to collect. Interior designers are meant to help people set up a background for their chosen lives and the process of decorating should be ongoing.

The common thread I've observed in good marriages is the loving, caring ways they treat each other. Lovers love to be together. They build each other up and are proud of their partner. I see partnerships where one mate encourages and reinforces the other privately and to close friends. While many couples enjoy sharing in the selection of things for their home, most often one person has more experience and style and the partner is rewarded by his or her mate with generous compliments. This mutual support

> Share in a love of home.

51

makes all the difference. Anita is now in medical school because her husband Paul was aware of her desire. Encouraged by Randy, June is studying at interior design school because her untrained talents working on her house in Memphis proved to be extraordinary. She is excited to learn and is considering working part time for a friend who has a shop.

Lovers respect the separateness of each other, therefore they encourage each other to explore individual interests. Lovers are not jealous or envious, so all the good fortune of a partner can be fully shared. When lovers are secure they have an abundance of love and it is natural to "let go" of the other and let things happen naturally. David is a successful lawyer and encouraged Kate to return to Vassar to get her degree after their three children were in high school. Lovers understand that timing changes circumstances but not love. Kate is now a research doctor and works sixteen hours a day. David is proud of Kate's accomplishments and when they are together they treasure their free time. They run together five mornings a week and vacation for several weeks in the summer in Europe on bicycles. Two of the three children are in medical school and one is in law school.

Lovers should always take care of their own needs first because when they do it is natural to act graciously toward each other. What would you most like to be doing? This question can lead to major life changes and has in many of my clients' lives. When couples communicate as lovers they are aware of different needs in their mate as circumstances change. It is the key to happiness of two people to know your own needs and to be able to express them. Self-sacrifice always boomerangs because it never makes the person feel whole. Doing things out of love and commitment brings pleasure in the process as well as satisfaction in the results.

Lovers don't play roles, lovers play together. I'm fortunate that I have a mate who helps me realize my dreams while he is realizing his, and we both contribute to making the process fun.

Lovers enjoy being helpful. They like to serve the one they love. When Connie was studying to take her architectural exam,

The key to a successful relationship is self-esteem.

You can change yourself but you can't change others.

Hugh tested her and they worked together putting together a model. Hugh is a minister who relies on Connie to critique his sermons. Nancy has an attractive antique shop and decorates, and her husband, a surgeon, helps her by going on buying trips and also does her company books.

Lovers make a constant effort to see that the needs of the other are met. Lydia, an archaeologist, was invited on a scholarly trip to Eygpt and her husband Edward was unable to leave his financial business. He encouraged her to go alone and now they are planning a future trip together. She says the trip was the experience of a lifetime. Loving couples expand each other, never keeping each other from exploring and growing into deeper knowledge.

Lovers prepare an attractive nest. The bedroom of a loving couple always has a pretty bed. Whether it is a four-poster, a bed with lovely bed hangings, or with a charming headboard, the bed is sacred and has attractive linen, pillows, and coverings. When a loving couple wants to spend time together, good reading lights are provided as well as good storage. Ideally a woman prefers her clothes closet to be private from her mate's. It has a different mood—different colors and smells. It's fun to dress and change clothes in privacy and then be able to make an appearance. The seating arrangements of a loving couple are intimate, so that two people can face each other (on sofas, love seats, or chairs) and be close enough to talk and easily be heard. One can feel the intimacy in a room that works for a loving couple. Both people's needs are met. Double sinks with raised countertops make shared bathroom time a mutually pleasant experience.

Where and how we live gives clues to our relationships. If a lover is concerned for his love, he will leave the bathroom neat and fresh. Lovers think of the other person's pleasure and happiness. Tidying up becomes a love act, a gesture of affection. When you make things nice for a love, it is fun for you.

Lovers pay attention, wanting the best for the other. At times it means sitting in a room together talking. Other times it means listening only. And often it is appropriate to share silences. Sue

"The essential elements . . . of the romantic spirit are curiosity and the love of beauty."
—*WALTER PATER*

53

and William have turned their living room into a music room and go there to enjoy the music playing on a good system. Lovers share "I've always wanted . . ." stories and help each other realize their dreams.

In the evenings you share together, create memorable hours. Plan ahead so you can go to the theater or a lecture, a concert or movie. Make a special point to go to a hard-to-get-into restaurant after the theater and then plan to relax an extra hour in bed together the next morning. Hours well lived together set the stage for future hours. Careful planning eliminates routine and disappointment. Then live your moments together, don't merely organize and plan for future events. In other words, savor an evening out and don't plan the next one at the dinner table but fully experience the present. On the spur of the moment, after two depressing days of rain, when the sun comes out, drop everything and go on a bike ride to enjoy the smells of spring and to experience rebirth and the burst of color. "Why not seize the pleasure at once?" Jane Austen inquires. "How often is happiness destroyed by preparation, foolish preparation!"

Within this private and uniquely personal bond, encourage each other to take necessary risks and move on from one well-lived chapter to the next. A young couple with two small children chose to give up a high-paying salary at an advertising agency because the husband really wanted to go to work for a TV network. The fact that his wife encouraged him made all the difference. Their financial sacrifices were shared and he became very successful as a television programmer. Welcome these necessary changes as opportunities for discovery and for creating a deeper feeling of partnership. The apartment next door to Mark and Anne became available and they talked it over and decided they'd like to buy it, break through the walls and double their space, even if it meant they'd be poor for years.

A marriage is a partnership in much the way two lawyers form a partnership. When both people pull their weight, more than 50 percent of the time it works. Within this healthy framework each partner can make mutually beneficial decisions according to each other's needs because of a profound respect for the other person's dignity and value as an individual.

In 1961, when I was nineteen and madly in love, it never occurred to me to keep my maiden name when I married. The women's liberation movement hadn't begun and it was the proper thing to do to take your husband's name. I feel differently now, especially for women with a career. During the twelve-year period of my first marriage, Doubleday agreed to publish my first book, I was writing articles for *Harper's Bazaar*, working on my second book, lecturing, and developing my interior design ability as well.

When I told my literary agent, Carl Brandt, that I would be remarrying, he quickly asked, "What's your future husband's name?"

"Peter Brown."

"Keep your name. Alexandra Brown is not your name as a writer, Alexandra Stoddard is." Peter was delighted that I chose to keep Stoddard as my professional name, and I love it because I have two Stoddard daughters. We tease Peter because whenever we have a family vote the Stoddard ladies can always outvote the one Brown! I believe a woman should keep her own identity when her instinct dictates her to do so. Our personal identity matters and is very connected with our self-esteem.

Be sure you feel comfortable about your name and politely let people know if they introduce you differently from the way you desire. The concept of a woman's having a personal identity is relatively new and people often make assumptions without thinking.

Asking "How do you like to be introduced?" is thoughtful because so often you can introduce someone who has been improperly introduced to you.

I was giving a lecture in North Carolina not long ago and my hotel accommodations were arranged by the company who hired

WIFE'S IDENTITY

"Self-confidence is the first requisite to great undertakings."
—SAMUEL JOHNSON

Relationships aren't automatic; they require conscious attention.

me to come and talk to their district sales managers. Peter was meeting with some lawyers and was promoting his new book on local television. Inadvertently we forgot to check at the desk to be sure our room was listed under our two separate names. Sure enough the next morning the breakfast tray arrived and Peter was handed the local newspaper by a cheerful and well-meaning waiter. "And I hope you have a nice day, Mr. Stoddard." Fortunately, Peter has a good sense of humor and laughed after the man left the room. This will happen—it's unavoidable—but it can be easily corrected.

EQUAL PARTNERS

We share our spirit with others.

When I was about to marry Peter, my first book, *Style for Living*, had been published. I had my design career, and my two lovely young daughters, Alexandra and Brooke, were six and four. Peter made an appointment with me so we could speak without interruption: we sat down and he told me he was marrying his lover, not a housekeeper. "I don't want you to show me love by darning my socks, ironing my underwear, or packing for me," Peter told me with great sincerity. "I love you for what you are and don't want you to change a thing for me." This was a dream come true.

We hired someone full-time as a day helper who took care of the girls when I was at the office and who also did the housework. The mere fact that I didn't have to prove anything to Peter domestically made me very happy. This freed me to concentrate on nesting and creating our new home. I had great mobility to go about my business doing what came naturally to me around the house; and I could do little things for him to show my affection.

My full-time career thrived with this freedom to be utterly spontaneous in the extra work I did around the house. I never felt my home responsibilities were a burden. Rather, it became a pleasant aspect of nesting and nurturing to do the little pretty things the spirit moved me to do and not feel guilty about others I did not do. Peter, in turn, was nourished by my exciting career and the way the apartment looked.

Lately, Peter has developed a ritual of bringing me juice and coffee in the morning. Of all his tender gestures, this gives me the most pleasure. I can stay in bed in the morning and write in my journal, I can read and do some writing in peace before my busy day begins. Life is constantly changing and Peter has changed gracefully with the circumstances.

We no longer have children at home to make breakfast for. Therefore it is no longer necessary to sit at the breakfast table to sip our coffee and juice. Until the girls left the nest we got up, set a pretty table, and made eggs, hot cereal, toast, juice, and hot chocolate, both of us eating a real breakfast, trying to set a good example. These were happy, memorable moments we enjoyed as a family, but things change. We are alone now, watching our weight on what we call our "diet for life" and a substantial breakfast isn't necessary; in a few hours we have a good lunch.

This role reversal of Peter bringing me juice and coffee after my getting the family breakfast for almost twenty years allows me a moment of time in the morning. Before I get up and get going, I can count on the accumulation of these moments each morning, rain or shine. They are a real gift. I know that wherever I've left off in my writing the day before, I can pick right up and stay in the flow. So more than the gesture of coffee and juice, this becomes an opportunity for me to have some private time alone to daydream. It frees me to utilize my dreams and thoughts fresh after a night's sleep, to organize my ideas for the day. I have a moment in which I can write a letter, read poetry, or make a "to do" list if that's what's on my mind.

Peter as the butler bringing me coffee and juice on a silver tray brings him pleasure because I'm always appreciative and it's a service of love at the beginning of a new day. This simple gesture is its own reward to him because it makes me so happy. It also gives him some puttering time in our pretty, sunny, pale-blue

"Confidence in others' honesty is no light testimony of one's own integrity."
—MONTAIGNE

kitchen. He can glance at the headlines of the *New York Times* and mist the gardenia leaves. I have a feeling that this mini-separation each morning is a blessing for both of us and a spiritual, rewarding time.

A man is the other side of woman; she is yin and he is yang. But a man and a woman are only half alive if they specialize in a purely masculine or a purely feminine role. A larger, more well-rounded mind bears the stamp of both. It is a huge mistake for men to be limited to "the rational," when their intuition can guide them the same way intuition guides women. As Peter jokingly says, "I'd far prefer arranging flowers to emptying garbage." I have a male client who grows orchids. Another male client hooks rugs. So often women have been brought up to "run the house" and they often *run a man out of the house* by not allowing him to co-decorate, co-cook, co-arrange flowers—and eventually co-anything.

I still know some women who have been conditioned to believe that a man doesn't belong in the kitchen. I think this is silly. Consider all the great male chefs throughout history. My daughter's boyfriend loves to cook for her. Men have a very secure place in the kitchen; after all, we share in the joy of eating, we should both share in "the joy of cooking." Our kitchen is a favorite room in our apartment. Aside from both of us cooking, often Peter puts on an apron and gathers together our brass pots, opens the bottle of Brasso, and polishes like crazy while I'm puttering. He regularly changes the water of our flower bouquets and cuts back the stems, rearranging the bouquets in smaller vases as needed. I've set aside a spot at one end of our kitchen where there is a collection of vases next to the sink so he can work and not be in my way while I'm cooking near the stove.

Our minister, Hugh Hildesley, loves the ritual of setting the table. I'm renovating two New York City kitchens for clients because the husbands are the chief cooks in the family and they want the kitchen to function more efficiently. One male cook insisted on a large double stainless steel sink so he's always assured a spot with running water. I have a female client who prepares the family's

> Tolerance requires absolute honesty.

joint income taxes for their accountant. She has her own private desk and it is an unwritten rule that her husband won't go rummaging in her files. She takes her task as family bookkeeper seriously. These small examples only show that the barriers have been broken in many male-female relationships. We're both equally busy. We're both equal. We have to work things out so that the work and responsibilities of the home—which is mutually enjoyed—are equitably distributed between two equal loving partners. We must remember that men are great decorators, entertainers, cooks, and gardeners and no place will be more rewarding than home to let these talents flourish. Offer encouragement.

The really happy couples forget male-female differentiations at home. When we are able to express all aspects of life we are far more creative and fulfilled. Encourage your mate to play a musical instrument or stencil the dining-room walls. I have a male client who loves to make miniature furniture for his daughter's dollhouse.

> Living Beautifully Together is the result of your personal dreams.

The most important ingredient in a marriage is mutual respect. Try never to take each other for granted. When you're with a person all the time you expose all sides of yourself. No matter how stable each individual may be, there are inevitable ups and downs in a marriage: one partner's behavior greatly affects the other's. Be sensitive that your patterns don't hurt your partner's feelings.

A young attractive blonde from Pittsburgh married a Wall Street lawyer and had a happy June honeymoon in Bermuda. Once at home in their Greenwich Village apartment they got into a routine of domestic life and returned to their jobs, but something bothered this radiant bride. Every morning Karen set a pretty table in the kitchen near the window using various wedding presents and they would have breakfast together. Meanwhile, David picked up the *New York Times* and devoured page after page. He came up for air only when he reached for his fresh-squeezed orange juice or freshly brewed coffee. One morning Karen asked her distracted husband

DON'T TAKE YOUR PARTNER FOR GRANTED

what kind of eggs he wanted and he mumbled, "Poached, please." Karen lovingly poached his eggs, basting them just the way he liked them, and there they sat. She fumed and sat tight-lipped watching the eggs get cold and hard. Of course he hadn't even noticed. His article in the A section was continued on D-16. Finally she burst up from the table. "Why did you tell me you want poached eggs if you're not going to eat them?" David, completely in his own world, dropped his *New York Times* and apologized, eating his cold eggs out of duty and guilt.

Was he inconsiderate not to put the newspaper down and have a few moments of conversation with his wife? Two minutes is all it would take. Or maybe she could adjust and read the paper too, and talk later in the day? David's newspaper became an emotional barrier between him and his bride. This was a hard transition for Karen, who had been spoiled by having his undivided attention during their coffee kisses and romantic hand-holding breakfasts together on their honeymoon.

We all have to tune out things that interfere with our ability to concentrate, but we should be careful to be thoughtful about when and where we exercise our powers of concentration. This particular lawyer wouldn't think of going to the office not having read the paper thoroughly; he reads not just because he feels he owes it to his clients to be informed (and his subway ride isn't long enough), he is in the daily habit of reading the morning paper with his breakfast and enjoys it. Karen rationally knows this but the fact that he was a million miles away still bothered her.

In a marriage it is necessary to talk things over and find ways both partners can have time to do what they need and choose to do, without inconveniencing each other.

If newspaper reading seems like an emotional tune-out, make a turnabout. Both can read the newspaper together and both whip up breakfast together. Or, create a game in which each partner takes turns making and serving breakfast. Because Peter and I both devour the morning newspaper and then clip out articles to save and send friends, we got the idea early on to have two newspapers delivered each weekday. This might seem like a huge luxury, but it makes for more pleasant mornings together and each of us can take our newspaper with us on our way to work or on a business trip. If I've finished my paper and have a daughter at home, I like to leave it for her to look through. Having two newspapers works well for our family.

Trust your intuition. It is your true wisdom.

If we accept that all of us have difficulty understanding the inner life of the people to whom we are closest, it helps us not to get upset when there are misunderstandings. No one fully understands his own emotions and all we can expect to accomplish is to really try to understand our partner by communicating well.

Often our consciousness is raised after we've hurt someone else's feelings. Try to be alert to what your spouse is experiencing. If he or she serves you a drink in a glass you don't like, let it go. Avoid being petulant because it may lead to anger. Ask your spouse how he or she feels about little things. Shall we have an early evening and go to bed and read? You might be saving your partner from overdoing and coming down with flu. By asking, you show your interest and express your care. What you want for dinner may not be what your mate desires. Don't assume, ask. I have a client who loves to cook and he wants company in his self-prepared feasts. Often his spouse, who constantly has to watch her waistline, wishes she could have soup and salad. A good idea is never to try to read your partner's mind or expect him to read yours. What you choose to watch on television might be a turn-off to your partner. Inquire. Maybe a video you rent would be better entertainment than watching what is available on scheduled programming.

If there are special shows you want to watch in the coming week, tell your mate of your intentions and it will free you both to do what you want. If one person doesn't want to watch a program and the other does, possibly you could record it and watch it at a mutually convenient time. All these nitty-gritty details of everyday

COMMUNI-
CATING

"Look with thine ears."
—WILLIAM SHAKESPEARE

life need to be worked out in order for you both to continue to feel good about yourselves. "What do you feel like doing tonight?" might give you a surprise answer. Listen carefully. While it is natural for two people to fall into patterns when they live together, make each day provide fresh opportunities for variety and adventure. Life is lived in a series of moments; create magical moments together each day.

Allow for fluctuations in your moods: provide for more spontaneous, serendipitous happenings. Because marriage can encompass the full range of experiences—sexual union, homemaking, childbearing, child rearing, travel, entertaining, caring for aging and ill parents, work, finances, and hobbies—you have a kaleidoscope of possibilities open to you each day. Plan wisely. Time passes unrelentingly whether you take action and plan your life well or not.

Take turns in who makes the decision. It's best to ask, "What movie would you like to go to?" "Where do you think we should go for our vacation next summer?" Just because you feel like going fishing and your spouse craves staying on the beach reading Jane Austen doesn't mean you're hopelessly incompatible. Don't assume. Ask. Just because you've always gone to the baseball game with the group doesn't mean your wife doesn't want to be invited. Provide options. Don't, on the other hand, assume someone is unhappy when sitting under the shade of a tree sipping lemonade, reading. Given options, we usually do pretty much what we want to do as long as we feel safe that we aren't hurting anyone. When you ask your partner a thoughtful question you show genuine concern. You are equal decision makers.

When you live with someone full-time you have an opportunity to open up and become more than a good listener; you can become a keen observer. For example, Melinda, a woman in her mid-forties, was having premenopausal problems and had been advised it might be wise to have a hysterectomy. She dreaded the possibility and was agonizing over the decision. Her choices were to go ahead with the operation requiring a six-to-eight-week recuperation period or tough it out and see whether the problem would work itself out. A difficult choice to make.

She was visibly upset but didn't want to complain. Her husband, Paul, noticing her anguish, volunteered to go with her to her doctor to discuss whether or not to have a hysterectomy. A huge weight appeared to lift from her shoulders. Her face relaxed. She was very touched. To see is to change things. Once he understood that his wife was hurting (and her hurting was intensified by her concern about *his* reaction to the changes going on in her body), he took action. She no longer had to carry the entire burden. Frightened of losing her femininity, she had someone with whom she could share the decision. She opened up and touched Paul as they talked and her fear seemed to take a backseat as she shared her anguish. Sharing divided her pain and multiplied her hope.

Listen well, observe, and work to develop a sensitivity to better understand the feelings, nuances, and emotions of your partner that aren't always spoken. Look for signals—sighs, frowns, body language, a change in personal habits—and be available. Silently your partner wants to be heard and understood without voicing negative sounds. Being loving and concerned doesn't make the problem go away, but it may make the concern for the problem lost its negative power. Be willing to put in the emotional energy necessary to see things through. When a situation seems painful and you feel afraid, share this. Help lighten the burden for your spouse by communicating your concern.

Melinda and Paul's appointment with the gynecologist proved to be helpful. They agreed together to delay surgery. Melinda feels Paul is rooting for her through the months ahead. Paul treated his wife with sensitivity, respect, and dignity—also with an awakened tenderness that helped turn her from feeling helplessly confused and sad to optimistic. An extra phone call during the day from Paul asking Melinda's how she's doing, a little extra affection, some compliments that are deserved—these little gestures help enormously. Pay attention and things have a way of working out.

BE SENSITIVE
TO AESTHETICS

---

*Beauty makes us feel
uplifted.*

---

*Make your point
without anger.*

Jane's husband had a habit of placing his trousers on the top of his high chest of drawers and closing the drawer so they couldn't fall down. This habit was automatic and Jane couldn't imagine why he couldn't hang up his trousers in his closet. She went to the hardware store and bought six extra trousers hangers and placed them neatly at one end of his closet rod. Nothing seemed to work. She would lie in bed at night and fume. She'd find herself looking up from her book, staring at those bloody trousers.

One night she got up out of bed, tiptoed over to the chest of drawers, and opened the top drawer a crack so the trousers slithered to the floor unnoticed by her husband, who was watching television. The next morning he was amazed. "My trousers are all wrinkled on the floor. This has never happened before." The next night when he came home from work he tried again—after all, he'd had this chest of drawers in his room growing up in New Jersey and it had never happened before that his pants ended up in a heap on the floor.

When it happened three nights in a row it dawned on him—he found the spare hangers and put them to use. Was it cruel of Jane to open the drawer slightly? Should she have yelled and screamed? Or gone over and hung them up in the closet herself every night? If she nagged he could get defensive and think he married a fishwife. Sometimes you have to do something unusual in order to get someone's attention, especially when they have a bad habit they're resisting eliminating.

Men like to air out their clothes but there should be some way to do this without turning the bedroom into a men's locker room. I personally loathe those racks men use to air out their smelly jackets. If a jacket is soaked with perspiration, it probably belongs at the dry cleaner. I went to a client's house several years ago and in the master bedroom I saw the husband's underwear being aired. If the shorts were spanking clean they would have been in a drawer, and if they were being aired, what conclusion could I draw? The drawer or hamper and no in-between! All personal necessities should be concealed from a spouse as much as possible. Bras, panties, stockings, when not on the body should not be visible in the bedroom. If there is a spare bedroom where a suit can hang on a shower rod overnight or a dressing room or even a spare closet where the door can stay ajar, that could be an alternative to the chaos and depressing sight in the bedroom. Even a spare hook in the laundry area can work. Your bedroom should be a peaceful, lovely place of grace, and it takes both people wanting it to be attractive to achieve success.

The recent Bureau of Census and Labor statistics indicate that 55.8 percent of all women are in the work force today. And according to a 1986 survey of 1,409 households, 84 percent of the household cleaning is still done by women. Even when a husband makes a huge effort to help out around the house, as well as to spend time with the children, the wife still holds the lion's share of responsibility for the operation of the household. In a study of 210 Virginia families, men were spending an average of 1.6 minutes a day on housekeeping. Let's hope some of these men's wives aren't working full-time and doing all the household work too.

DIVISION OF LABOR

A woman has always had to try harder than her husband to make everything work out, even though she may have a job outside the house and share paying for their joint living expenses. This is largely due to entrenched attitudes which change slowly. There remains a double standard even in the best situations.

Because men have inherited the hunter/killer instincts from their Stone Age ancestors, they often feel uncomfortable coming home and doing little nurturing domestic chores, fussing around the house. When someone is uncomfortable, nothing happens. A woman makes a warm nest for her hunter-husband and dependent children and, in addition, often works to bring in an extra income. Somehow she still finds time to cultivate her mind and create beauty.

This is a tall task. We need as much help and understanding from our partner as possible. But women can help by learning to invite their partner into these domestic areas and do it with a sense of sharing the fun. Buy your spouse a handsome chef's apron and get down to work together. In half the time the chores are behind you.

PARENTS AS PARTNERS

Because so many married people want to have children it is difficult not to discuss parenting when talking of dividing up the work between a wife and husband.

Parenting has definitely become more of a partnership, but when two parents are both off on a business trip and their child has a high fever, the wife usually comes home. The attitude that the man's career is paramount is hard to erase. The idea that the wife's job is a pleasant second income runs deep, and few men want to be reminded that they are not the sole breadwinners. In many dual-career marriages, men and women are contributing equally to the financial operations of their joint lives. When a woman earns more than her husband this can be a cause for tension. There are many excellent examples of marriages in which the husband's emotional and physical support has been so valuable that the wife has been able to accept a job of great importance—Sandra Day O'Connor and Margaret Thatcher come to mind. The traditional sexist roles continue to swing into a new perspective, liberating both men and women.

If you choose a career that demands that you be away a great deal, or if you work under constant deadlines, maybe you will decide you don't want to have children. Often we wake up to the truth that something we wanted isn't in line with the reality of our lives. No one can tell you what you want or what is right for you because other people only draw from their own experience, which might be limited. How much effort you are willing to give to accomplish your goals depends on your individual drive. Nurturing a family

Family love is the linchpin.

66

is not a woman's only focus anymore even though it may well be her number one priority.

An attractive couple with two demanding careers waited to have a child until quite late because the woman wanted to be assured of an equally binding commitment from her spouse that he would be a co-parent. It took time for him to come to terms with her "terms" and once he did she got pregnant.

Each situation is unique in ways only you and your spouse can understand. Certainly the less pressure your spouse puts on you, the freer you are to explore your own projects in a positive climate of self-discovery. Be fairly private about how you manage to divide up the labor. It's one thing to adore your spouse bringing you coffee and juice and quite another to go around telling your friends he washes out your stockings. At best you'll get jealousy and envy from friends if you have a very supportive spouse who carries a fair share of the domestic burdens. At worst you might get an earful about how you should be handling such matters yourself.

If you don't want a houseboy for a husband and he doesn't want a housekeeper for a wife, you both need to work things out as you go along, helping as much as you can. Don't give anyone the opportunity to have an opinion on your private affairs. It is none of their business, and I know from experience to keep many secrets. We have an expression in our family: "Play dumb." Work things out between you. Enjoy the process of give-and-take. If there are things you both dread doing, give up something else so you can hire someone to come do them for you. Do everything that gives you positive reinforcement. I love to iron and polish silver, but I get no kicks from the laundry room and I'd rather live in a broom-swept beach shack than have to vacuum up dust from a carpet. We have bare wooden floors. I adore waxing and polishing wood.

I know a young couple who divide up the housework differently each week, and with the money they save they go out to the movies and supper. When you do something yourself you know the scope of the job, how long it takes to complete a task, and whether there

Work out your own salvation.

are satisfactions from your accomplishments. Listen to music, help each other—this too will pass! Do what you do with a sense of pleasure. After all, it's your floor you're mopping!

THE WIFE'S BUSINESS TRIPS

It takes a man with a great deal of self-assurance to be a real support to his wife's career especially when it is inconvenient. When the girls were relatively young I took on an exciting decorating assignment, working on an eighteenth-century Directoire *hôtel particulier* in the heart of Paris. Opportunities like this don't happen every day for an American designer, and I knew I couldn't turn this down without regretting it later. Peter was extremely supportive and he took care of the girls in the evenings when the housekeeper left the apartment.

Every evening when I called home the girls were giggly happy and I received a cheerful report from Peter that things were running smoothly. This eliminated my feelings of guilt and allowed me to feel the thrill of my work there to its maximum potential.

Peter highly recommends husbands' going on their wives' business trips, even though it requires juggling schedules and being secure while your wife is in charge. When we photographed the Paris house several years later he came over and assisted us in taking pictures. I have a friend who travels with his wife and helps her research her books. When two people love each other and want to be together, things can often be worked out.

MAKE YOUR OWN TRAVEL PLANS

When I was working on the interior design of a bank in Texas a few years ago I was sent on a buying trip through the Texas hill country, conveniently planned during the bluebonnet season in May. Luck was with us—Peter was also invited. It was all planned so we'd have a real Texas experience, going to local fairs and antique sales, seeing old architecture, eating local food. I flew down a few days ahead of Peter, who had business in New York and was to join us on the weekend. I'd flown to Dallas where we went to a crafts fair, then on to Austin and San Antonio.

Joining me were the bank president, the project controller and his wife, the landscape architect and his wife, and a board member who had been a good friend and client for over twenty years. The proud Texans made ideal arrangements so we Northerners could experience Texas at its best. Friday night we would stay in the oldest stone house in the charming little town of Fredericksburg. We arranged in Dallas for a college student to pick Peter up at the airport and drive him to Fredericksburg. Everything was meticulously planned.

We were having a jolly time, enjoying ourselves enormously, waiting for Peter by a big warm fire. After patiently waiting an hour after his estimated time of arrival I began to worry, and because the old stone house didn't have a telephone, one of my friends went with me to the gas station nearby so we could call the airline and see if there had been a delay. We learned there had been a thunderstorm in New York and that Peter's flight was delayed. He managed to get another flight on a different airline, but since he couldn't communicate with us, no one was there to meet him when he arrived.

Because of the confusion the storm caused, he was exhausted when he arrived in Dallas and when he didn't see anyone there to pick him up (it didn't occur to him he was at a different airline than was agreed on originally) Peter took a taxi to a nearby hotel.

We tried to read his mind, and after several calls we reached Peter at an airport hotel. He was enraged "by this whole mess." We arranged for the porter on duty to drive Peter to Fredericksburg the next morning. Dripping wet from the rain, I left the public telephone crying, "How could something so innocent become such a nightmare?"

Staying in a house with no telephone is obviously rare in our electronic age, but that's part of the charm of staying in an old house. As with mountain climbing, picnics, or camping, there is a special peacefulness we all seek from living simply. When I look back on this experience, the lesson learned is to make your own travel plans. Don't let your wife or secretary make them for you. When you do it yourself and things get messed up, you don't have anyone to blame but yourself.

PRIVATE TIME ALONE AND WITH YOUR MATE

Regularly make an effort to plan private time when you can be together, receptive to see and hear what's on each other's mind. The quality of special times when you can sit and be attentive allows both of you time to relax, unwind, and appreciate each other. You should also make dates with yourself to have private time. I've noticed a tendency among couples living together for one to entertain the other when they're together. Constant little interruptions, chitchat, and comments can be frustrating if you really seek a private moment when you can accomplish a task.

Tell your mate, "I need some private time. Let's get together in an hour." That way each of you can focus on personal things without any misunderstanding that one isn't paying attention to the other. That will happen in one hour. Now, there's private time for each partner.

We all have goals, things to do, and can't just sit around the house night after night being "on call." It's important for us at times not to have interruptions, not from children nor even from a spouse. Create times free from outside demands, when you can daydream or try to accomplish something creative. Thinking about something and giving yourself the necessary time releases anxiety and allows a flow of clear thinking. By making real dates with yourself as well as with your mate, you are fully utilizing the free time you have. Figure out a rhythm that works well. I prefer having private time alone so I can organize myself, putter around a bit, straighten things out around me—and in my mind—and then sit down to have a visit. What you want to avoid is having too much of one without the other. Keep a healthy balance between togetherness and private time at home. You and your partner will antic-ipate your "dates" when they follow mini separations, even if you've been in the same room for your private time but worlds apart.

Peter and I have found great pleasure in reading together. We read in bed in the morning and at night. Friends tease us because our bed has so many pillows, but it is a great luxury to have lots of big pillows to lean against when reading in bed. We have functional halogen reading lamps so we have strong light. We read after work, sitting in the living room or the library, and a large part of our weekends—whether we're home or away—we spend reading. We find we are always drawn more intimately together in this process. We take turns reading out loud, sharing passages. We may buy a paperback copy of a favorite book so we can both reread it togther and discuss it. Reading is our avocation and reading together in-creases our pleasure. The gentle, spontaneous interruptions to read a few lines or share an insight are welcome. When we are reading very different kinds of books we share the most interesting parts. Whenever one of us reads a book we are certain the other will enjoy, we enthusiastically communicate this belief and so far our instincts have been right. Peter recommended *In Search of Excellence* to me, which I thoroughly enjoyed. I introduced him to Rilke's *Letters to a Young Poet*.

We read book reviews and decide what new books to buy and read. Because we later use books we've read for reference, we are careful to keep books on a particular subject matter together—we have shelves of books about the law and several shelves of books on Impressionism. I had bookcases built in our bedroom along one whole wall for books we intend to read or reread. They include some of our favorites and some new books by or about favorite authors we plan to read in the near future. Because reading brings

READING TOGETHER

"I love to lose myself in other men's minds."
—*CHARLES LAMB*

"The future is purchased by the present."
—*SAMUEL JOHNSON*

us such pleasure and nurtures us mutually, we have enjoyed putting together a library that reflects our personalities and interests.

I have friends who enjoy taking turns reading short stories and fairy tales aloud. Another couple enjoys it when the man reads Sherlock Holmes stories to his wife. If I'm driving I'll ask Peter to read me something from the newspaper. Often when I'm cooking he'll read to me. Most of us remember being read to by our parents when we were small and that happy memory never leaves us.

TIME TOGETHER, TIME APART EACH WEEK

Alice is an optimist and expects a great deal from life. She possesses an unusual amount of energy, and as a fashion designer has gained recognition and respect in a highly competitive field. Joseph is a lawyer and a pessimist, and has low energy. He works grueling hours at the office trying to meet the quotas of chargeable time his partners expect of him, and when he arrives home he is spent. All he wants is to be left alone in peace, have a drink, and read. This has been the pattern and it's not a happy reality for Alice, who wants to talk, share her experiences, and have some fun after a full, productive day.

The way Alice worked it out was to have a talk, listening to his discouragement about the pressure he was under and how exhausting the rat race is. She, on the other hand, got her views across and told him she expected more excitement from their marriage. She looks forward to her evenings off and wants to make plans to go out, see friends, go to the theater, go dancing, and enjoy the benefits of living in an exciting city. Alice and Joseph spent an entire evening talking, and because neither one judged or blamed the other, they were mutually understanding of the differences in their individual needs. They agreed to make definite dates to be together, both at home and out. Alice now goes to the ballet with a friend. Each week the schedule varies, but there is a plan and Alice knows what to expect. Instead of being unhappy with each other, they've decided how they'll spend their times separately and together. Alice

"The goodness that thou mayest do this day, do it."
—*GEOFFREY CHAUCER*

encouraged Joseph to play tennis on Thursday evenings in a men's doubles game and she has joined a book club that meets the same evening.

Once a month on Tuesday evenings they go to the opera together. It's easy because they have season tickets. They plan it for the year and go automatically. Sunday afternoons they enjoy going to their local museum, and take turns in deciding what exhibit to see. They also enjoy the short movies offered at the museum, which they learn about from their membership newsletter.

MONEY

The principles of money are the same whether you are budgeting a weekly allowance or running a business. When I was sixteen, my aunt took my sister, a cousin, and me around the world. This eye-opening journey to thirty-two cities in thirteen different countries irrevocably changed my thinking about money. Having seen, in India, the agony of extreme poverty and also seeing the corruption of excessive wealth, I've grown to realize that money is power and that power can be used both constructively and destructively.

At this time, when I first experienced the extremes between the "haves" and the "have-nots" I was on a full scholarship at art school in New York City and had to borrow two hundred dollars from a friend for the trip. My aunt arranged for us to stay in fifty-cents-a-night youth hostels (the dollar went farther in those days), and our biggest extravagance was going over to the Cairo Hotel from our hostel and paying seventy-five cents for a cup of cappuccino. This was in December 1959, and I can remember the taste of the cinnamon on the roof of my mouth and still savor the memory of the richness of the whipped cream. I have never had cappuccino without remembering being in Cairo on a December morning feeling like a millionaire savoring each precious sip.

Developing a positive attitude about money is a tool that is essential in a good marriage. In all partnerships money must be discussed regularly. Set up some general guidelines that are clearly

"Riches are chiefly good because they give us time."
—*CHARLES LAMB*

understood by both partners. Abide by them strictly. Financial irresponsibility is a form of ignorance and causes great insecurity and pain. We all like to make plans and money security is essential. Our hopes, dreams, and fantasies are connected with money because it is the commodity we use to translate ideas into reality.

Fifty years ago, in an era when it was usually the husband who was the sole provider, my mother saved money. She took money out of the food budget and hid it in the closet so she could accumulate enough to buy a hat, splurge on a store-bought cake, buy a new car blanket. Everything was tightly budgeted, allowing her no leeway for the item that didn't fall into the category of dire necessity. Peter's mother did the same: her weakness was jewelry. Who could afford jewelry in those Depression years?

Money is power and the one who has it likes to control it. If you and your partner agree that only one person will actually earn money while the other person provides the right climate for the success of the job, the money should be shared fairly with no strings.

Separation of certain funds between partners is essential. I've read that some marriage counselors think it is a sign that the marriage is getting better when husbands and wives join their accounts. I disagree. How can a wife buy a present for her spouse and get any pleasure from it if she is merely writing a check from a joint account? There must be a few secrets between spouses. How much you pay for a necktie for your spouse and how much it costs you to have your hair streaked and the price you pay for a new dress should be your private business.

Money does matter. Although money alone cannot make us happy, it can, when used properly, bring freedom and "scatter joy." I am a great admirer of Brooke Astor, who has done so much for the public good with the Astor Foundation. When she was being interviewed on "60 Minutes" by Mike Wallace, he asked her how many gardeners she has at her house in Westchester. She paused as if to visualize each one and said "I have seven." And in Maine? She reflected thoughtfully and answered, "I think the same amount." Wallace probed, "I'd hate to think what the annual—"

Brooke Astor interrupted. "Very high." Wallace inquired, "Don't you feel guilty about being so rich?" She said, "I feel, of course, extraordinarily lucky. I'm terribly lucky to have all this." Wallace asked her, "Why do you love Maine so?" Mrs. Astor answered, "Because it has mountains and it has the sea, both. And I can climb a mountain and sit on the top of a mountain and look out and see the sparkling sea and all the rocks and marvelous fir trees and you realize this, whether I'm here or not, you know, the line of Aiken which says 'like bread that for our daily fare is broken, the eternal loveliness before us spread.' And I feel here it all is going on night and day whether I'm here or not. There is something very, very extraordinary about it." Wallace inquired further, "And you feel . . . Somehow I get the sense—maybe you got it from your Chinese experience—a kind of oneness with nature." Brooke Astor's philosophy poured forth. "A oneness with nature. Well, the Chinese think everything is alive, this [chair] is alive because it was a tree once. And I feel my house, for instance, when I come back to it I have to go 'round and give it love. I say, 'I love you, I love you, I love all the chairs, I love all . . .' I go 'round and put my arms around the trees." Then she went on to explain that she had been raised to give away 15 percent of her money and she has always done that.

Money is freedom. Once we are able to provide food, clothing, shelter, and education for ourselves and our children, we are free. I have observed people of great wealth agonize over files of paperwork, involving financial advisers, insurance agents, lawyers, bankers, accountants, bookkeepers, household help, cooks, gardeners. Often they aren't aware of the trap their wealth has become. Being enormously wealthy has the potential of consuming one's time and energy, which is tantamount to losing one's freedom.

Keep your life simple. If you have more money than you can handle with ease, get help. The whole point of having money is to make life fuller. Thoreau suggests we make our needs few so that we can live rich. When you feel bogged down by your financial decisions, write a check to your school or university, write a large

Desire change and you will welcome risk.

"Simplify, simplify."
—HENRY DAVID THOREAU

donation to your place of worship. Support your local shelter for the homeless. If your situation is the reverse, if you feel you are drowning financially, save your loose change and give it to the poor. There is always someone less fortunate and when you feel low, giving a portion of the little you have brings your perspective back.

I have never committed myself to buying a weekend house. I was forty years old before I bought my first car and I've now sold it. Who needs a car when you live in the city if there's no country house to drive to? I appreciate the little luxuries I can afford because we have deliberately kept our lifestyle simple. I feel comfortable being able to pay bills on time, to enjoy saving a little for a rainy day, and to have money to give away to needy people and organizations.

Money—its value, its power, the way people treat it—is highly personal and is usually the number-one source of real difficulties in a marriage. Communication about finances is essential. How much money do you give away to charities? How much do you budget for household help and operating expenses? How much money do you spend on your clothes, restaurants, little luxuries, travel, vacations? If a woman is home earnestly clipping out coupons and buying things on sale while her husband is a big shot flying around the world first-class, she has cause for resentment. To maintain our dignity, we need both money and financial freedom. When money is an issue, it's far better to talk it out, not shout it out. Make a list of suggestions for improvements you can both make, noting areas where you feel expenses have gotten out of line.

Try never to be a victim of other people's spending habits. I remember when I was first married, we went out to dinner with some tennis friends one night. We knew the restaurant was expensive but we decided we would splurge. We ordered ground steak and our friends had steak with béarnaise sauce. They ordered escargots, soufflés, special side dishes of asparagus and hollandaise sauce. We "weren't that hungry." They began with a few scotch and waters, had a bottle of good French wine with the meal; we had Perrier water with a twist. He ended with a cigar and brandy, she had a crème de menthe. We had a lump in our throats that wouldn't go away. We were kicking each other under the table and for a good reason: when the bill came we were asked to fork over half the amount which was over twice as much as we had budgeted.

It took us weeks of sacrificing to make up the money we foolishly lost that night. We were victims of someone else's spree. We learned our lesson the hard way. No one has any idea of someone else's financial situation. Fifty-fifty seems fair, but under the circumstancs of our near poverty and their grand style of living, it wasn't. It was our mistake to have gotten in over our heads with big spenders. Terms should have been spelled out at the beginning so there were no surprises.

Philosophers for thousands of years have written that the best experiences in life are free. Joy is not in things, but inside us. "He who knows he has enough is rich," observed Lao-tzu.

Regardless of the amount of your budget, having some guidelines helps maintain financial order and control. Each partner should contribute to the pool according to his or her ability. The proportion doesn't have to be equal, but the commitment should be.

HOUSEHOLD BUDGET

Americans have shifted over the past several decades from saving to spending, saving only 3.8 percent of their income, which is not enough. Consumer credit outstanding has risen over the past fifteen years to 19.4 percent of the average American's income.

Set up seven budget categories: 1) *Necessities*—Food, shelter, and clothing, and whatever else is essential to you: eduation, medical needs, telephone, transportation, insurance, exercise. Be sure your taxes will be covered, if you work free-lance. Try to allow 70 percent of your total household budget for your necessities. 2) *Decorating and art*—Allow 6 percent. 3) *Nonessentials*—Records, books, household help, stationery, bubble bath, luxury takeout food, plants and flowers = 5 percent. 4) *Gift giving, entertaining, and holidays*—Allow 5 percent. 5) *Vacations and travel*—7 percent. 6) *Savings*—5 percent. 7) *Miscellaneous*—2 percent. Make this your goal and work toward this balance.

Live with this budget for six months and then review it. See where you have to cut back spending, see how quickly you can accumulate savings when you have a plan. Be strict with yourself at first; education expenses are enormous. You have to plan well for a future. Prices go up rapidly. Compare your bills for heat, telephone, and food. But once you have things under control, ease up a bit and enjoy yourself. I have a friend who lives in an old farmhouse in Vermont and her needs are so simple she feels rich: she need never concern herself over food prices. Her family eats well by growing their own fruits and vegetables, and baking their own bread.

Reward yourselves with a treat if you haven't dipped into your savings for a three-month period. Saving brings freedom from the anxiety financial pressures can cause. The best way never to be a victim is to maintain a balanced household budget.

DECORATING

Effort is self-fulfilling.

Certainly one of the most pleasurable aspects of living with someone is nesting. When both partners work, decorating is often done in their free time. Decorating is a process that begins once you have a place of your own and it should continue throughout your lifetime. Men have always shown great sensitivity to the arts and enjoy being equal partners in the exciting creative decisions of decorating their home. The pitch of a chair, the length of the arm, the depth and height of the seat, the swivel, the fabric pattern and color make a difference.

A client married a petite lady and we used the same-style chair in their dressing room in two different scales—a small upholstered chair for her and a large model for him. The height of a counter matters. Recently I renovated a kitchen where we raised the countertop around the bar sink area where the husband works, and kept the rest of the countertops standard height for his wife, who is five feet three inches tall. The height of the gooseneck faucet set should be determined not by appearance alone but also by what you clean in the sink. Flower vases need to be considered. The gooseneck should swivel so that it can be out of the way when not needed. Likewise, the color of the oak floors matters, the way the windows pivot or tilt make a difference; the style of the living room mantel affects your mood and sense of delight. All these decisions define us—they represent us and illustrate our point of view. The corner detail on the kitchen counters, the selection of tiles, the color of the grouting, the shape of a valance, the way the knob feels to the hand—all these decisions are important and should be shared. When they are, the results will show the breadth of both personalities, merging two solutions that can be far more imaginative than if only one heart and mind were focusing on the workings of the home.

Both people must establish an equal presence in the home. We all express our personalities where we live and our home can be a sanctuary where we translate our spiritual values into our physical surroundings. If we value beauty, our home will reflect this spirit.

Certainly we enjoy ourselves more in a place we have had a hand in creating. I remember with great fondness when my mother, the daughter of a Boston shipbuilder, laid wide-plank oak floorboards in a farmhouse we owned in upper New York State. My mother probably inherited her love of woodworking from her father. She would pound those nails into the wood with great precision and after a few rows were firmly in place, she'd lean back, stretch, and smile down at her gorgeous effort.

While I've never laid a hardwood floor, I have sanded, scraped, plastered, and painted. I've set tiles, made curtains and slipcovers, and I have done needlework, embroidery, smocking, knitting, and worked with painted finishes. I've even tried my hand at gilding. Eudora Welty once said, "We see human thought and feeling best and clearest by seeing it through something that our hands have made." Aside from the obvious financial advantages of doing some

"Life was meant to be lived."
—ELEANOR ROOSEVELT

physical things oneself, there are two other, more subtle benefits. First, when you personally do the work you are being creative, putting your own finishing touches to things so you can have them just the way you want them. Second, when you focus on what you want and then make the effort to make it happen, you feel more alive and more in control.

I've observed that when clients have enough money to remove themselves from the physical work of decorating and homemaking there is a tendency to pick away at those who are hired to help them. The truth is, few people we hire will ever care as much as we do. When we spend time actually doing some of the manual labor ourselves, we feel more at one with our environment because our human hands have worked to create something that didn't exist before.

Let me give you an example: Last summer Peter and I refinished the butcher-block countertops in our kitchen. We used Zip-Strip to clean off the polyurethane sealer and then we hand-sanded the maple until it was smooth and a lovely natural color. We'd been to a fish restaurant where the tabletops were natural maple and they looked wonderful. When we inquired how they were cared for we learned that the grease and oil were removed with Ajax on a hot sponge. We wanted to achieve this scrubbed-down look and went to work the following weekend. It was a lot of work, yet I enjoyed sharing this project with Peter, and we treated ourselves to a late lunch after we'd made a dent in the job. I couldn't have hired someone who would have cared so much and put as much energy into the project.

"To know oneself . . .
assert oneself."
—ALBERT CAMUS

Now these counters are ours. The hours we spend in our kitchen are more pleasant and we know how to make the wood look and feel the way we like it.

Don't wait to be given permission to do home improvements yourself. Select some area in your house or apartment that is up-setting to you and attack it. I have clients who are painting their studio apartment "atmosphere blue" so the walls, as they put it, will seem to "expand into infinity." Another couple painted their living room peach with white trim and stenciled flowers in shades of green around the ceiling cornice molding. (They bought the stencil kit at a Janovic Plaza paint store in New York.)

Select projects you will enjoy doing. Everyone begins as an amateur, and experience helps us to perfect our skills. I guarantee you that any project you personally perform along with your partner will bond you closer to each other and closer to your home.

Just as the men and women in the Stone Age ornamented their caves, going beyond what was purely utilitarian, we satisfy our yearnings to be distinctive by carving out a very personal place for our private world of retreat. If one of us is denied full involvement in this process, it takes away the fullness of the pleasure possible at home. Anyone who says they don't have time to be part of the creative process of homemaking is saying they don't have time to live. Many people get caught in a situation in which they are so locked into long, grueling hours at the office, they haven't the strength to come home at night to work or make decorating decisions. "You decide, it doesn't matter to me," is a tune-out. Home is not just a place to sleep, home is where we house our souls. A keen one-on-one relationship with everything at home is essential to balance our lives. Everything matters—the way a towel absorbs, the design of a wine rack, the color of the living room, the texture of the sofa material, the sound of the chimes in the clock.

Each partner must take an equal interest in and be mutually committed to turning their house or apartment into their dream environment. No one can dream your dreams for you, not even a loving partner.

Share in all decisions that pertain to where you live. Make dates to go scouting for wanted items. Set priorities and agree on them so you have clear-cut goals. Never let money interfere with aesthetic decisions and sharing. Even if one of you is paying for a painting or a four-poster bed, you both will look at the painting and sleep in the bed. Often the one who pays the bills has veto power. I strenuously disapprove of this and have known couples who have strained their marriage because the one with the money became,

"All who joy would win
Must share it,—
Happiness was born a twin."
—GEORGE GORDON,
LORD BYRON

"Men . . . cannot be pleased against their will."
—SAMUEL JOHNSON

in effect, the boss. You both should work toward decisions that are mutually rewarding and meaningful.

I've observed that couples tend to grow more alike with time and they tend to get into similar patterns. They might both drink scotch, play golf, collect hunting prints. Although initially we might be attracted to someone who is quite different, over time we influence each other and tastes meld together. When two people come from similar backgrounds, this is especially true.

Ideally your living room should be a statement about your love partnership, not a visual autobiography of one with the other acting as a guest in the house. Being a guest is never permanent. In a lasting relationship it is essential that the two partners create a symbiotic and aesthetic result. When this is achieved it gives both people a sense of belonging, connection, and roots.

When I married Peter I moved into his Park Avenue apartment. We both had living-room furniture. Mrs. Brown came to visit us as soon as we got settled and she inquired, "How did you ever decide whose furniture to use?" Peter laughed, "Eleanor, it was very simple. As Alexandra's furniture came up the front elevator mine went down the back elevator." This is not entirely true, but I made some major changes in the living room simply because I needed to make my presence known in a room that had lived a former life with another wife.

The way to synthesize two different styles is to envision what you want the result to be and then edit and draw from the best each of you has to offer. With the exception of very young couples, few of us begin our partnership from scratch. We each had a life beforehand. We might have traveled light, yet we still have possessions we are attached to and it is these things that will tell personal stories about who each of us is and where we've been.

While many couples share in the decorating of every room, each person may have one room that is his or hers alone and can be decorated entirely by that person. In Paris, my clients, both Ph.D.s, each have their own library. An anthropologist has her own

Ultimately we strive for balance.

studio and next door her husband has his sitting room. An added advantage to this method is that the room can be a real haven to retreat to when one wants to be alone; the walls will seem to caress you because they are, in a real sense, you.

Sacrifice things your mate absolutely loathes in your shared rooms. In the case of sentimental inherited furniture, compromise. I have a client who hates his wife's father's Louis XV desk, yet she can't part with it and it is too grand and formal to be used in her small study. The desk is a real issue. I suggested the desk be picked up to be refinished, cleaned up, have the missing veneer replaced and the brass mounts cleaned and after it was in mint condition, put back in the living room so they could take a fresh look at it. They agreed. The desk came back looking magnificent and the husband admits he really likes the desk now. "It used to depress me, it was so beat-up." Problem solved.

Years ago Peter was going through an Italian garden period. I look back on it now with a sense of humor, but at the time I was upset. He had sold his Federal house in Southport, Connecticut, and must have been very sentimental about losing his garden. He was suddenly drawn to and purchased some garden statuary—little chubby cupids all made of stone. This fascinated me only briefly—we don't have a garden! We live in an apartment and there is no place for these bulky stone objects. One cupid had a dear face and she lived in a bathroom for a while until I eventually complained. Peter agreed to store them in our basement locker. I hope we will remember that we own these characters if and when we ever buy a house and have a garden.

If connecting and communicating are the key to all good relationships, I strongly suggest sharing in every decision that affects the appearance of your shared nest. After a certain age, few of us like surprises. While we can't always change the way we look, we can agree to the way our home will look and feel. I believe in equal veto power. If you find a French Provincial end table in an antique shop on your way home from work, go together and have a serious

"A wise man will make more opportunities than he finds."
—FRANCIS BACON

look at it. This way you can both have personal satisfaction if you buy it and live with it. It becomes a piece of furniture "we" purchased, not one "he" or "she" bought alone.

Never let an interior decorator intimidate you into decisions that aren't comfortable for both of you. Never let a decorator break up or interfere with your aesthetic partnership. If you do seek help from a professional, before you have your first meeting have a clear sense of the way you want to live and how you want things to look and feel. A designer's look is not necessarily yours and it is possible you could be in the hands of someone who is trying out a new trend or style on you. After all, you pay, so get what you want.

Decorators, interior designers, and architects are useful only if they listen to you and try to interpret your individual ideas. You will be influenced by a designer or any other competent professional, so interview carefully and always maintain a firm grip on the direction in which you are headed. Many couples who make their home a top priority have been able to make wise and imaginative decisions together without outside help. I believe my profession is useful as long as we serve your joint personal needs, helping you to translate your philosophy of life into a beautiful home. When we do our job well enough for you to forget you ever had any help (because everything is a personal statement of all the positive beautiful things you value) we have done our job and should leave the job site!

EXTRAVA-
GANCES
AND LUXURIES

Keeping a check on fixed expenses allows more freedom to spend a certain amount of money on unnecessary fun things as well as on exciting times. Living within your income, spending a little less than you earn, provides funds for unbudgeted items—an extra trip, a piece of jewelry, a new fountain pen, a marbleized file box from the Mediterranean Shop in New York, a dinner party, a hand-embroidered nightgown, an art book, a clock or watch, a flat of geraniums, a new tennis racquet, dinner and theater, a facial, a suit made to order, a new suitcase, or a silk bathrobe. The value we get from such pleasures far outweighs the money we spend. Money well-managed allows for extravagances and little luxuries.

I overheard a college student complaining to her friends at a coffee shop that her parents have two beautiful houses "because they consider real estate a good investment. All their money goes into those darn houses. I wish they'd consider my brother and me good investments and take us skiing over Christmas vacation."

A woman who loves to paint and is exceptionally sensitive to beauty lives with an investment banker. She longed for a Roger Mühl painting they'd seen at an opening at the David Findlay (Sr.) Galleries where they met the artist. Steve loved it too but said they couldn't afford it. "We have the money but all our money has to be invested where it earns interest. I'm trying to build my portfolio. A painting, no matter how beautiful, just sits there on the wall."

Steve has legal training and never loses an argument. Florence brooded until she decided to take action. She borrowed some money from her father to buy this picture which she couldn't get out of her mind and agreed to pay him back within five years. She went to the gallery without telling Steve and purchased the painting. Her delight was ineffable. She was proud she had the guts to follow her instinct and find a way to own the painting. Steve came home from the office one evening to discover the painting over the mantel in the living room. He was pleasantly surprised. Florence still felt her partner was stingy—he earned a big salary, whereas her part-time teaching job didn't pay that well. She spent a great deal of time at home and her environment meant a great deal to her. One winter evening they were sitting by the fire and Florence caught Steve gazing intently at the painting, studying it as if with a heightened awareness of its mystery and grace.

Florence had "won"; she'd raised Steve's consciousness. Half in jest she began to giggle. "If you stare into the painting with any more intensity I'll charge *you* interest!" Steve hugged Florence and asked her how many more payments she owed her father. Florence

Give good and memorable times together.

"He gives twice that gives quickly."
—Latin proverb

wouldn't tell, but seeing his keen interest suggested they go to the gallery and look at paintings together. Steve bought one by another artist they both liked, Pierre Leiseur, which led him to understand the value of living with art and beauty every day (not to mention the possible increase in value of these paintings—far beyond interest from the bank!).

When we earn our own money, we get pleasure from treating ourselves, our mates, our children, our friends, to luxuries when the spirit moves us. I think money should be used, not locked up. If we are happiest when we keep our lives simple, enjoying what we have as we go along, savoring the moments, creating wonderful memories, taking advantage of the opportunities that come to us, we must be comfortable with the attitude that our richness is in what we do to enjoy our money, not in its accumulation.

If living rich and dying poor is frowned upon by money managers, it can make for a beautiful life day-to-day. You don't have to buy art to appreciate beauty. On a student's budget a poster, a print, or an art postcard of a favorite Matisse is equally thrilling. Just this morning as I sat at my writing desk, I selected a postcard of a botanical drawing of a tulip; each day I change the postcard I have on a little stand. Whether you have forty cents to spend or four thousand dollars, the sense of celebrating *now* is a necessary element to learn in abundance. The attitudes we have about living and spending are often closely parallel. Don't be afraid to splurge. Remember to buy the hyacinth over the loaf of bread (provided, as Thoreau would say, that you are not actually starving) because the hyacinth will feed your soul.

One young couple has the worst arguments over money. Henry hates to spend and lives with the fear that he will lose his job and be down-and-out. Donna wants to live attractively and understands the value of spending money on their apartment. She works for a decorating magazine and goes on photographic shoots where she sees a constant array of beautiful objects she can purchase at reasonable prices for their apartment. One evening after working all day at a photography session under the pressure of a tight deadline, Donna was bushed and yet quite excited. She was completely taken with a little eighteenth-century pine child's potty concealed inside a table which she could use as an end table in their living room. She could open up the top and insert a blue-and-white spatterwork bowl and fill it up with sweet-smelling peach potpourri. She loved the color of the wood, the grain, the sturdiness.

"Henry, I've fallen in love with this little piece of furniture and I think we should buy it. I can get it for a very good price." Henry moped around, pacing. "We don't need it." Donna was exhausted and getting fed up. "Henry, I have psychological needs as well as physical needs. Here's a perfect spot for the table, right at the end of our sofa. But even if there weren't a perfect spot I could find fifty places to put this charming little table. Someday we'll have a house and each room will need furniture. Can't you see I really am attached to this charming piece?" Henry coolly suggested, "If you're *that* excited about something we have no need for, buy it out of your free-lance money." Donna did buy it, and Henry grew fond of it and reimbursed her for his share.

The definition of a luxury or extravagance is something you don't need, rather something you desire out of an emotional attachment. The moral of this story is always to trust your instinct. If you don't, you'll end up resenting someone who held you back. Trust yourself. We never regret what we do when it comes from our hearts—we regret the things we don't do.

I remember finding a pair of pottery dolls in Athens twenty-five years ago and they spoke to me. They were made by a well-known potter in Marousi and were quite expensive. I struggled with my decision not to indulge, and agreed not to buy them even though I believed in my heart I should. I left the store feeling sad—not in a spoiled way, but more as though I had lost two friends, the dolls. My husband and I were with some Greek friends and Elene ran out of the shop with a box. "A present for you to remember your trip."

"Surprised by joy."
—WILLIAM WORDSWORTH

Thrilled, I realized they were meant for me. They are now, all these years later, on a Greek marble-top tavern table in front of a huge window in our kitchen.

Another time I didn't follow my instinct, we were in the South of France on our way to visit a friend and we stumbled upon a little antique shop on a lonely road to Grasse. I found a table that was meant to be mine but it cost $250, and in 1961 that was like $2,500 to us now. I let it go and was haunted by its beauty. We traveled on to Italy and sitting on the terrace of our hotel in Florence overlooking the Arno River something clicked. "The table. We need to buy the table." I cabled and a little less than a year later my treasure arrived. This remains the single most treasured possession of my life. I write my books sitting at this table and it is where we eat.

We rarely regret what we do when we follow our instincts. The saddest words in any language are "what might have been." I don't like wasting money, but I believe in spending it well.

GOING OUT TO DINNER

A woman from Ohio married into one of the wealthiest families in America and in the course of the first dozen years of marriage gave birth to five children and acquired four houses. Each house is equipped with a full-time cook and cook's helper, plus, of course, a butler and a string of maids and gardeners. Comparisons are always odious but sometimes amusing and help us to gain perspective. I live in one spot—an apartment with a modest kitchen and no help other than a part-time cleaning lady. Now that the children are grown, Peter and I love trying different restaurants. This has become a passionate hobby—so much so that Peter published an international restaurant guide, *Guide Select Gastronomique*.

One afternoon this woman inquired, "Going out again? You must spend a lot of money on restaurants." I had a good laugh to myself. "I guess we do. When we go out to restaurants it's the cook's night off." I wondered briefly what it cost her husband to

"Moments big as years!"
—JOHN KEATS

have eight people working for them full-time, preparing, cooking, serving, and cleaning up in four different houses!

My passion for eating in restaurants became intense when I was a teenager on my trip around the world. All the restaurants we went to were inexpensive because my aunt's salary as an international social worker was modest. I can still remember so many of the meals we enjoyed over that three-month period thirty years ago. There was a great deal of experimentation: I used chopsticks and my fingers, I ate raw fish in Japan and pigeon in Cairo. Each country we visited had its own distinct cuisine. I remember the smell of honey bread in Greece, and the spinach stuffed in phyllo pastry called spanakopeta we'd get from street vendors, the curry puffs in India and the sweet-and-sour curry from Burma.

Now, living in New York, we can travel around the world without leaving Manhattan by going to restaurants with national and regional food. We choose among Southwest, Cajun, Creole, and Tex-Mex. We eat food from India, Greece, Japan, China, France, Mexico, and Italy. We enjoy the rich variety of taste treats available to us in New York City and feel that the money we spend going out to eat is a luxury we appreciate. Realizing every time what a treat it is to go out to dinner, to be served a delicious meal someone else prepares, serves, and cleans up makes each time a cause for celebration. Cheers!

> We never regret what we do when it comes from our hearts; we regret the things we don't do.

PRESENTS

We get such personal pleasure from giving presents. It is never inappropriate to give a present to your partner—no matter how valuable—as long as it is freely given with no strings.

When in doubt, give a present. People adore a little show of affection, and the special events—holidays, anniversaries, and birthdays—are times when we work up high expectations. A present requires thinking ahead, caring and understanding about the other person's feelings, knowing what will please.

Intimate couples should mark their calendar weeks in advance so they can start thinking what to give each other for special occasions. If you decide to make something that requires time away from the person you're giving it to, think well in advance. I am always touched by presents I receive that are engraved. They seem romantic and the sentiment will last forever. Whenever we are given by our partner something that is engraved we know we were thought of weeks before the date we received our gift.

Recently I was admiring a little girl at the beach with lovely curls and a chubby set of arms actively playing in the sand. I sat next to her and we patted the sand together. She was shy but enjoyed my company. She had no toys, only a beach full of glorious sand and water. She found a scrap of silver paper, actually a piece of gum wrapper, and she tore off a piece and handed it to me. I thanked her and she repeated her ritual three more times. Each time I thanked her and when she had nothing I gave her back one piece at a time. There was a pleasant rhythm of exchange. When we both had presents I got up to leave and said good-bye. The first word I heard from this adorable little child was "bye," which she repeated several times, adding a wave with a tight fist as she clutched her treasured silver paper. I have mine before me at my writing table, resting in a dish filled with sand from the beach. Both of us were united in a bond. This child instinctively knew about giving presents. She gave me what she had.

Whenever we give, it comes back to us; genuine giving always delights the giver and the receiver. Rollo May writes in *Love and Will* about "the love act" in which there is "the tenderness which comes out of an awareness of the other's needs and desires and the nuances of his feelings. The experience of tenderness emerges from the fact that two persons, longing, as all individuals do, to overcome the separateness and isolation to which we are heir because we are individuals, can participate in a relationship that, for the moment, we are not two isolated selves but a union." A sharing takes place which brings on a new beginning.

Don't give your mate a present for the house—a blender, an appliance, a toolbox—just because the house needs supplies. Give

---

Be motivated by beauty.

something that is personally meaningful. One partner might adore a well-equipped toolbox while another would prefer a piece of jewelry. I know a couple who give each other tiny colorful eighteenth-century enameled boxes made in South Staffordshire for special occasions; the boxes have a few words of sentiment on the top. For Valentine's Day Melissa received a pale-blue box with white birds perching on red hearts. In the middle it says:

LOVE
& Live
HAPPY

On the occasion of Donald's fiftieth birthday Maureen gave him a dark-blue box with the words "A Pledge of Love." Little antique gift boxes like these are reproduced today in England and can be found in gift and specialty shops and jewelry stores around the country. Enjoy an opportunity to be intimate and tender. Think way in advance what your mate might want and encourage some solid hints to help you decide.

Once when we were on vacation, I was writing and Peter came up to me. He bent down, kissed me, and announced, "I have a present for you." I smiled, "I love presents," and I looked up to discover a bouquet of field flowers he'd picked while on a walk in the woods. Get in the habit of giving little surprise gifts of love to your partner. It could be a book, a violet plant, a new handkerchief or a tie. Everyone loves a little unexpected present. Bring home some Oil of Olay or a few magazines, some perfume or after-shave lotion, a good bottle of port, or a box of pretty stationery. You both want each other to have these little niceties and when you thoughtfully select some and give them to your partner you are doubling the pleasure the item can bring.

Special-event presents are command performances when you live with someone. If you save up you can give serious presents that can be enjoyed for years. One man gave his wife a piece of jewelry every anniversary, and after thirty-three years of marriage she has quite a collection.

Consider giving your partner a lovely leather belt with a gold buckle or some enamel cuff links. Peter gives me earrings for my birthdays—anything from Tiffany's Angela Cummings gold-and-stone designs to Herbert Givenchy's fun costume earrings to wear when dressing up in the evenings. I love to give Peter books—and he generously adds to my collection of art books each birthday, Christmas, and anniversary. We usually give each other more than one present on special events. One year I gave Peter a swatch of fabrics with a promise note for him to be measured for custom-made shirts. Things to wear—clothes, jewelry, scent—are intimate, loving presents. When you are in stores together, observe what kinds of things your mate is attracted to and encourage open discussions about personal preferences. One year I saved up and splurged on a yellow cashmere sweater for Peter only to discover he doesn't like cashmere. Who doesn't like cashmere? Peter!

Cynthia gave her husband a battery-operated, rich blue travel clock from Tiffany's. Peter loves to give me a fountain pen on special occasions. One of my favorite presents is a silver picture frame with a picture marking a special family event.

Give your partner a wonderful red-and-white-striped cotton bathrobe from Ralph Lauren or some pajamas from Paul Stuart in New York. Indulge in some Turnbull & Asser silk neckties and colorful silk handkerchiefs from Neiman-Marcus. Replace a worn-out wallet for your mate with a new one from Mark Cross. Buy your mate a new Dopp kit for bathroom items. Buy a lizard handbag at Chanel and put a slim tube of her favorite peony shade of lipstick inside along with a love note. Even if none of these stores is nearby, most have catalogs from which you can order by mail. Always make the effort and purchase something that can be gift-wrapped. In the unlikely event something needs to be exchanged, you can go together and make it a pleasant, shared time.

One couple from Chicago celebrated their first wedding anniversary at home having an elegant dinner for two. Jane gave Philip a season ticket to the opera and Philip gave Jane a reservation for two weeks later for dinner at a classic French restaurant. Give a promissory note for ten back rubs or a pledge you'll make Sunday brunch once a month. Giving the promise of good times can be more meaningful than things. The sheer spontaneity makes wonderful surprise gifts twice as wonderful. Even without spending a lot of money, you can show through kind acts that you love your mate.

CHECKING DATE BOOKS

For a couple with dual careers and children, getting dates straight is crucial. How often we hurt each other inadvertently. "I wish you had told me!" a husband yelled at his wife. Frustrated, she shouted back, "I told you a dozen times the school play was March eighth. What's wrong with you? Brian is your son, too." Sit together once a week, preferably at a set time, say Monday morning at breakfast, and review your dates for the week. Flip ahead for the far-off dates that have a way of suddenly being upon you.

There is always the girl or boy inside us.

You are two busy people with different demands and a variety of meetings, children's activities, social engagements, family obligations, community work, business trips, and deadlines. This requires careful examination of all the dates in order to do what you mutually consider priorities and still have enough pauses in your calendar so you don't overdo. You need enough free spaces in your date books for time alone when you can be in charge of the choices you make and what you will plan to do.

The slightest misunderstanding can hurt the harmony that you both seek. I used to pride myself on remembering dates, but I've realized it's better to free your mind for more creative tasks. Instead, write everything down. I have so many dates, including all my clients' scheduling, that I totally rely on what I put in my date book. I feel secure when everything is in writing.

If it's too complicated to have all the information in a portable date book (like a Filofax) that you can bring to the breakfast table, then I suggest a telephone date when you can both share what you've committed to in your work, what's coming up that needs an RSVP and what activities—like a lecture, class, theater, concert, or ballet—that require money sent in time to assure seats. You can see the value of a conference, even over the telephone: You can get your dates straight and make more pleasurable dates for the two of you.

WRITE DAILY NOTES

Communicating well on a daily basis is thoughtful and prevents unnecessary stress. It allows a loved one to know where you are and how to reach you if needed. We have a rule in our household that we always leave a note on the front hall table whenever we leave the apartment. It's nice when someone walks through the front door to a welcoming note instead of silence, wondering where everyone is.

Being informed saves worry.

Even if you are just walking the dog or picking up some watercress, it's comforting for the other person to be informed. It's a sign of caring. Keep a pad of paper and pencils in a drawer in the front hall table or some self-stick removable 3-inch-square notepads. They now come in white, green, pink, and blue as well as yellow. Avoid the misunderstandings that are inevitable with two pressured schedules. It's difficult enough for us to remember our own appointments and meetings without having to remember our spouse's schedule each day. As Samuel Johnson wisely stated, "We need to be reminded, not informed." Hearing the screaming of a spouse, "I told you I was going to Dr. Lombard's at six forty-five. What's wrong with you?" can easily be avoided. When you are informed, you are free to be calm and go about your business. Once you're in this habit, like writing down a telephone message for a spouse, it becomes automatic.

When you remain married to someone for a long time you both will have some sadness to face. No matter how well you may be able to handle it, you'll have to experience the pain of losses—loss of life, loss of health, loss of freedom. When you are sad because your mother died you know how awful it is for someone to tell you "It'll get better. Each days gets easier." That is not the news you want to hear. Learning to let go is never easy.

Grieving is a necessary passage and having someone tell you that in three weeks you can hop, skip, and jump over your sadness diminishes your ability to love and become part of another person. The writer Madeleine L'Engle's husband of forty years died several years ago, and she wrote of death: "Unless it is murder, accident, suicide—[death] is not an unnatural part of the whole journey of life. Death cannot take away anything that two lovers have had. Grief can be acute, and yet clean."

I like being in touch with my feelings and resent anyone's interfering with my grieving. Whatever the loss—a spouse, a parent, sibling, child, friend, a job, money, a breast, or a dog—let those you love grieve their loss. The best way to help a sad partner is constantly to reinforce your love for him. A friendly pat on the back as you brush by, holding hands, being there patiently with a handkerchief while your partner cries and tells you stories—all are expressions of love. Bringing a cold washcloth and soothing your spouse's eyes, offering a back rub, sending flowers with a dear note, splurging on a quiet romantic dinner for two—these are positive reinforcements and show great kindness and understanding. Peter took me to Caneel Bay the day after my mother's funeral. It was just what I needed and it's still appreciated.

During turbulent emotional situations when someone you deeply love is feeling acute pain and anguish, hire someone to come do the laundry. Do the cooking and car pool yourself for a week. Dont' offer, simply do. Never say to a sad spouse, "Come on now, snap out of it."

After my mother died, my dear friend John Bowen Coburn, then the Bishop of Massachusetts, wrote me that he has never gotten over the death of his mother. "I thank God for that." His words are so true and wise. I know I will never get over my mother's death. The truth is we shouldn't try to get over things; rather, it is good to live them fully, accepting them the best way we can and becoming changed by them. If we want to go walking in the woods alone, a spouse must let us go; if we want to light a candle in a cathedral, we should feel good about doing that.

"For everything you have missed, you have gained something else."
—*RALPH WALDO EMERSON*

If you both enjoy praying together, that is an added thing you can do together; as long as it works, don't stop. But it is important not to judge people's character and spiritual dimension by the style in which they choose to practice higher values of faith. Allow freedom without judgment. Spirituality is practiced in different ways every hour of each day.

FEMININE SPIRITUALITY

Madeleine L'Engle wrote that "women are going to have to be strong enough and patient enough to teach men. To attempt anything—music, love, art—is to risk failure, and that takes a kind of courage I believe to be uniquely feminine. This openness to change, interdependence, questions with no easy answers, vulnerability, and risk is the feminine spirituality that is desperately needed if the human race is to reach the year 2002." Men and women can explore far more meaningful relationships together if they dwell more in the right side of the brain which allows for holistic experiences.

L'Engle realized she had been taught from a masculine point of view as a child: "Be brave; do not cry; do not show emotions; be morally virtuous; do it yourself; never ask for help; be good and obedient and the world will be perfect." But her instincts drew her intuitively to daydreaming during class and writing stories when she should have been doing homework. "We were allowed no time for daydreaming. Daydreaming was suspect. 'What *are* you doing?' "

L'Engle learned that the root word for heal, health, whole and hold, is hale, as in "hale and hearty." "If we are *healed* we are healthy; if we are healthy we are whole; if we are whole we are holy—that is all being holy means." We should seek (until we find) wholeness first in ourselves and then with our partners.

No intimate relationship sustains itself over a long time without a few waves and storms. There are periods when it is beneficial to both partners to have some time apart. It is highly individual how much intimacy and togetherness a couple wants and needs. Whatever feels good is healthy and no one else can judge this for you. Closeness is between two people. Keep it personal. Distance— when you are merely taking a break, not running away from a problem—can allow the heart to grow fonder.

TIME APART

It is a wonderful feeling actually to miss someone you live with all the time. Often when you do get away you gain necessary perspective on your own life, strengthening your inner resources which help keep your relationship fresh and vital.

I've always felt fortunate to have business trips that transport me to another place where I get an entirely different vantage point of my home, children, and husband. More and more women are discovering the fun of moving around and broadening their frame of reference. An authentic relationship must allow this space. Remember, we tend to instinctively do what we want to do and when we're kept from this freedom it invariably backfires.

Peter and I have friends who will celebrate their fiftieth wedding anniversary this winter, and they have worked things out so they can remain married and in love. For them, temporary geographical separation is the answer. He spends most of his time in Colorado where he thrives on the low humidity and crisp mountain air, enjoying hiking, cutting wood, cooking, looking after his farm, going to town, fishing. He is full of energy and his spirits are up when he is there. His wife, on the other hand, loves her life in

Antigua where she grew up. She goes to Colorado to the mountains with David quite regularly but she misses the water.

Instead of continuous togetherness with one spouse suffering, they lovingly agreed to separate for longer periods and come together for meaningful visits. They have found a way to make their loving each other work out equally well for both of them in their later years. They write letters and call each other on the phone. Separation isn't for everyone, of course, but it is right for this wise and compassionate couple. We had dinner with them recently, and both were so happy to be together that they radiated appreciation of each other in their loving glances.

Then there are couples who live together and yet seemingly separate lives. Who am I to judge another couple's happiness? Everyone's relationship has a different itinerary. When we get to know each other well and feel good about ourselves, we tend to want to be there for the other person emotionally if not always physically. We work these things out. In times of great joy and sorrow, being together is important. When you've established a close bond, physical separation can bring an element of depth because you feel so close in spirit. Worrying that your spouse will be unfaithful to you while away is a complete waste of time and an insult to your partner's integrity.

"One crowded hour
of glorious life
Is worth an age
without a name."
—THOMAS OSBERT
MORDAUNT

VACATIONS

You can tell a great deal about people by the way they spend their leisure time. When two partners plan their joint vacation it can work well to have each spouse responsible for the planning of every other trip. Peter and I do this: if it's my turn to be the trip planner I do research, come up with an idea of where we should go, make all the arrangements for where to stay, where to eat, what to see and do.

One of our favorite trips was to Charleston, South Carolina, in April, where we saw lovely gardens in full bloom and looked through the historic houses. This was my trip to plan so I asked friends of ours who moved there ten years ago when the gardens would be at their peak. Once I got that information I called our travel agent who made our flight reservations. When we travel, our vacation begins when we make our plans. Anticipation is such a big part of the pleasure of an adventure. And we save money by making definite plans ahead of time.

For the plane ride down I packed a simple picnic for two. We had shrimp cocktail followed by cold roast chicken breasts and half an avocado pear with French dressing. Our delicious supper on board was a luxury and it is so easy to do when you plan ahead. A good picnic turns coach into first class.

We stayed at the Mill House in Charleston, which is centrally located. Even though we have friends who offered to put us up, we prefer not to be houseguests on these mini-vacations because we want to be able to come and go as we choose and have privacy. When you are a houseguest there are restrictions on your mobility and romance. When you have only a few days to see the sights and be alone together, freedom is essential. We always specify a light-colored, cheerful room with a view. (Once when Brooke and I were in Paris in March we were placed in a dark-blue room, and we found that between the rainy, damp weather and jet lag, the dark room acted as a sleep chamber. We found ourselves napping half the trip away.)

Our friends arranged for a guide to take us around to thirteen houses during our stay. And they gave a party for us so we saw lots of friends. Southerners really know how to be gracious.

Our four-day trip is not over even though it took place over a year ago. We have photographs in a scrapbook. Most of all, we have memories that sweeten our lives and we are expanded by the beauty, the charm, the warmth of friends. I bought some quilts in Charleston to add to my quilt collection. I came up with a solution to one of my decorating jobs as I toured a house on the Battery. (We needed to find a way to encase a 14-inch steel beam after removing a wall between two spaces, and fluted Doric columns on either side of a door to a historic house gave me the idea to use classical columns—one to hide the beam and the other for symmetry.)

Peter planned an equally wonderful trip for us in New Orleans. Charleston and New Orleans rank high on our list—along with San Francisco—of favorite American cities to visit.

We have friends who keep travel logs, and they can go back to the same room in a little inn and have dinner at a neighboring restaurant where they had grilled trout caught from the stream twenty yards from their terrace table.

Experienced travelers keep meticulous records of their own trips, take notes of friends' suggestions, and do a great deal of research. Bali is a romantic, primitive island in Indonesia, but you don't go there for the beach or water. Bermuda has far better beaches in the summer, fall, and spring. Where to sail, where to go camping, where to hike can't always be discovered through the Chamber of Commerce. Know why you want to go to a specific place and what you want to do with your time there.

You can go to Venice without studying Palladian architecture and you can go salmon fishing and not have to rough it. If you have the money for the trip you have countless options; the world is large and rewarding. Vacations don't have to be ruined by spending all your time inside Gothic churches or buying local souvenirs. Maybe you'd rather go to the island of Mykonos and hang out in blue-and-white cafés by the water and enjoy living there for a few weeks. It is perfectly possible you will both be excited about a spot for entirely different reasons. You like to go to Caneel Bay to swim, snorkel, photograph the exotic and colorful tropical flowers, read, eat luxuriously, and be in bed by 9:30. He likes going there to work on a book and sail. One partner goes exploring, the other shopping. You choose a place that allows each of you satisfactions.

Not every vacation has to be long and expensive. One dual-career couple I know takes a mini-vacation together in New England in October to experience the wonders of nature's changing palette, staying in inns along the way and antiquing—a restful, short vacation.

"I've taken my fun
where I've found it."
—RUDYARD KIPLING

"Into the midst of
things."
—HORACE

You can even plan a trip around an important art exhibition. Peter and I flew to Dallas to see the Bonnard exhibition and stayed in The Mansion at Turtle Creek. An extra bonus was a delightful reunion with good friends.

One of my favorite vacations is to take off without going away. Be a tourist in your own town. Stay in a hotel or inn where you live—no transportation expenses, no frustrating delays. Peter and I have done this on several occasions in New York and enjoyed ourselves thoroughly. Years ago, when I was eight months pregnant with Alexandra, my former husband and I were having a most pleasant dinner out. We'd spent the day painting the nursery and didn't miss the fumes. It occurred to me quite spontaneously how much fun it would be to go back and spend the night where we'd gone on our wedding night—a hotel that just happened to be around the corner from our Italian restaurant. We were both game and registered at the front desk of the Hotel St. Moritz on Central Park South, requesting a room overlooking Central Park if possible. The hotel lobby didn't seem that crowded and the registration was almost complete when the bell captain inquired where our luggage was. We looked at each other and giggled, and I blurted out, "We have no luggage." With an air of disdain we were told, "We're sorry. We don't accept guests without luggage." This man was uninformed as to our status or didn't have much of a sense of humor. My stomach was enormous, we were an old married couple there for a one-night stand.

The ultimate luxury is taking a weekend vacation without leaving your house or apartment. Firm ground rules must be established so that it works as effectively as if you'd closed the door and left your everyday life behind. At certain times of the year, in the winter when it tends to be gray and dark, this kind of weekend trip can be most rejuvenating to your spirit. First, treat where you live as a hotel. Chances are you will find more creature comforts at home than in any hotel room in the world. Arrange well in advance to have the window cleaner come. Luxuriate with supplies of fresh towels, soaps, body lotions, and powder from Caswell-Massey.

"Worth seeing? yes; but not worth going to see."
—SAMUEL JOHNSON

Splurge on fresh flowers, flowering plants, and scented candles. Remind yourself that you have no jet lag, no lost travel time, no travel expense.

Before you "don't go away," bring home a fresh batch of magazines, call your local florist, and send your spouse flowers with a card saying, "I hope you enjoy your stay." Buy your partner a bathrobe or a nightshirt as a romantic gesture. Stock your refrigerator as a hotel minibar with your personally selected delicacies, cheese, champagne, wine, beer, mineral water, and fruit juice ahead of time. Polish a silver or brass tray and lay out dainty linen cocktail napkins. Set up two pretty breakfast trays, complete with linen tray covers and napkins. Confine yourselves to your bedroom, sitting room, bath, and kitchen, as though you were in a huge, expensive suite. Turn off the phone.

You've set the stage. Think how magnificent it is not to have to unpack your clothes for the weekend—they're all ironed and you have your entire wardrobe to choose from.

Plan a rest, a leisurely bath, love, a cool drink, make a reservation in a hard-to-get-into restaurant for "after nine" which normally is too late. Take what seems forever to dress. This is your vacation. Luxuriate, rediscover each other, look, listen, touch, laugh, love.

Saturday morning, flip a coin to see who brings in the coffee, juice, croissants, and marmalade. Everything is prepared ahead, with matching trays. Stay in bed until you've read the paper and magazines and have a plan for the day. Don't do anything domestic except rinsing your glasses and dishes and loosely spreading over your bed. Don't stir until at least noon. Stroll to a museum, have a late lunch, go to a movie, window-shop. Go back to your "luxury suite," repeat your Friday-evening fun, select a different restaurant—dress up—and go out on a big date. When you call a top restaurant, inquire, "Do you possibly have a cancellation for two on the late side tonight?" We find we can usually get in if we're willing to go late. By Sunday evening you'll be glad to be home; you won't have travel delays, you won't have to unpack, and you

> You are the only one who can give yourself the gift of time.

will have discovered firsthand that there is no better place than home.

I firmly believe in each partner's having the freedom to take separate trips in the course of the calendar year. If you give yourself two weeks out of fifty, that is 4 percent of your time apart and I'm sure it will be time well spent. Career women and businessmen take trips for their work. If you don't have a job you should still be free to choose to do something for yourself either alone or with a friend. Women should take the initiative to plan what they want to do, where they want to go, and not have their time apart be when they're left alone because their spouse is away on a business trip.

It's healthy being personally responsible for yourself and not feeling guilty about taking time to see an old friend or go to a spa or on a ski trip. Just knowing you have an allowance of fourteen days to spread over 365 gives you a sense of control over your life.

My friend Ann left her two-year-old son and husband to go to Houston to visit old premarriage friends for a three-day weekend. They stayed up late talking, went shopping, caught up on gossip, and had lots of laughs. She came home to her happy-to-see-her husband and son and she loved the feeling of missing them. When you're with someone all the time and you go away, you both will think of each other often and it allows you the space to appreciate what you have.

I have a friend who takes her time away at a favorite little inn in Virginia. She has room service the first evening and reads herself to sleep. Saturday she luxuriates over an elegant light breakfast, reading, sipping coffee, jotting notes in her journal, daydreaming. "I love Ron so much more Sunday night after missing him and loving missing him. Having two days without conversation, only contemplation, is magical. It's like a spa for the mind."

Going to a spa can be a transforming experience. Jennifer went for a week to a spa outside San Francisco and lost inches all over but gained self-esteem and a sense of love for herself. Her husband went scuba diving at the same time and they reunited like young lovers exuding a joie de vivre, excited to tell their stories.

So spend some time with a favorite aunt, go see your godmother in Florida, or take a trip to Washington for a three-day seminar on Impressionist art. What are you going to do with your fourteen days this year?

TOUCHING

There is nothing more soothing and loving than a gentle caress, a hug, a pat on the fanny or the back. This tenderness, these affectionate caresses, are love in action. Americans tend to think of bodily contact more in terms of sex or foreplay to sex than affection. The Puritans disapproved of touching because it was sensual. I try to make all the areas of my life as sensual as possible. Tender loving touches can reassure, communicate, and soothe. There is no substitute for this physical demonstration of affection.

I remember as a little girl my older brother brushing my hair and how wonderful that felt. I, in turn, enjoyed brushing and braiding my daughters' hair.

People who are touched a great deal in infancy tend to be better adjusted and have higher I.Q.s than those less fortunate babies who are not touched and nurtured at birth. We should continue to caress and lovingly touch each other throughout our lives.

When you marry, you should enjoy touching the person you're going to be with for the rest of your life. Hugging, kissing, touching toes in bed, rubbing each other's back, petting—these gestures are instinctive to lovers.

But everyone has a different degree of personal space which should be respected. An acquaintance was in an automobile accident and miraculously survived what looked like a totally wrecked car that a Mack truck had hit broadside. Other than being black and blue all over and in a state of shock, Joan experienced no broken bones or any permanent injury. When I was with her shortly after the accident, she said, "I can't just lie in bed. All I do is feel the pain and I have nothing to distract me."

I asked her if she was getting massages to ease her pain. "No, I am far too modest to have a stranger touch me. I'll be okay." I felt sorry that she couldn't use massage for medicinal purposes, even if she was socially conditioned to resist this kind of experience. Within an hour or so after Alexandra was born in New York's Lenox Hill Hospital by natural childbirth, there was a nurse giving me a back rub.

Everything is growing increasingly impersonal as computers and other machines replace the warmth of the human touch. We could gain a great deal of richness in our relationships with others by communicating better through touch. If we were touched frequently as infants we probably find touching part of our regular vocabulary. If we feel uncomfortable being touched but want to do it more, just be aware that it's fun and natural and honestly feels good.

EROS AND SEX

In the Western tradition, there are four kinds of love: sex, eros, philia, and agape. Dr. Rollo May in his extraordinary book about sex and civilization, *Love and Will*, stated, "Every human experience of authentic love is a blending, in varying proportions, of these four. We begin with sex not only because that is where our society begins, but also because that is where every man's biological existence begins as well. Each of us owes his being to the fact that at some moment in history a man and a woman leapt the gap, in T. S. Eliot's words, 'between the desire and the spasm.' Regardless of how much sex may be banalized in our society, it still remains the power of procreation, the drive which perpetuates the race, the source at once of the human being's most intense pleasure and his most pervasive anxiety . . . and, when allied with eros, it can lift him out of his despondency into orbits of ecstasy. . . . It is a strange thing in our society—what goes into building a relationship—the sharing of tastes, fantasies, dreams, hopes for the future, and fears from the past—seems to make people more shy and vulnerable than going to bed with each other." As May points out, people are more wary of the tenderness that goes with psychological and spiritual nakedness than they are of the physical nakedness of sexual intimacy.

Dr. May observed that for some people sex has become increasingly meaningless. As it became easily available, people settled for "love without passion" and "sex without feeling." He states, ". . . the sexual form of love—lowest common denominator on the ladder of salvation—understandably became our preoccupation; for sex, as rooted in man's inescapable biology, seems always dependable to give at least a facsimile of love. But sex, too, has become Western man's test and burden more than his salvation."

Sex, without eros, is a pattern of neurophysical functions—what you do with organs, not what you do with your essence. "Eros" says May, "is the yearning in man which leads him to dedicate himself to seeking *arete*, the noble and good life. . . . Sex is a need, but eros is a desire. . . . It is this urge for union with the partner that is the occasion for human tenderness. Eros is the longing to establish union, full relationship."

I believe we should focus on the passion of eros, which always drives us to transcend ourselves through desire. When we concentrate on eros, sex will regain its power and mystery. Sex then becomes an instrument bringing us ecstasy.

"I LOVE YOU" Hearing tender words regularly is comforting, and a little romance each day reinforces the love that is the foundation of a married relationship. All through this book we've been talking about love as action, the small daily acts that express our love. When me make the extra effort to expose ourselves emotionally and express our sweet side, the loving feelings we have are communicated. Our lives become smoother and stronger, the rough times fewer.

None of us ever feels enough love. You can't have too much. If your own style is to have a kiss on the cheek as your code for "I love you," be sure you kiss that cheek a lot! Love has no calories, isn't subject to sales tax, and costs only your energy and investment in intimacy.

Tell your love "I love you" and you will always get a tender, loving reply. Look into the eyes of your love and you will see tenderness returned. Both of you experience grace by this simple, powerful act. "I love you" is unqualified. We don't say "I'll love you if you clean out your closet" or "I'll love you if you walk the dog." "I love you" means I want to reinforce and nurture you because I love and adore you.

Twenty Points to Remember

1.
STRESS

Each of us had our own capacity for handling stress. When we live with someone we should be aware that we will each handle stress differently. Stress is healthy as long as we don't become overwhelmed and burn out. Hard work is not stressful. Losing control over your life is.

Keep your life simple.

When our lives become unbalanced we temporarily lose our effectiveness. We work harder but get *less* done. Everything becomes a major effort; we do too much and don't enjoy quality or the process. We have to be able to walk away to be unaccountable. We have to know when we've overdone. Do something for yourself. Don't lose control and become somebody you'd rather not be around because you're under too much stress. Ease up.

When you can't handle too much of a load those around you also suffer. Men realize there is no such thing as a superwoman. There are times to push yourself and times to pamper yourself. No matter who you are or how "super" you are, there are still only twenty-four hours a day, distributed among us evenly. If a woman handles the finances, the decorating, takes care of the children, does the cleaning, has a job, a social life, and cooks the meals, she won't have time for hobbies, nurturing friendships, reading real literature, or daydreaming. Life should have certain spaces to pause, reflect, let things happen spontaneously. Don't always press. Handling stress requires the right attitude.

Here are some stress reducers:

- *Don't just be on time, be early.*

  If you get to your appointment with a few minutes to spare, you'll have time to collect your thoughts, have a few deep breaths, make a few notes to yourself, and arrived poised and in control. You'll be more effective and have more energy and higher self-esteem.

■ *Make dates with yourself.*
Plan ahead and mark your calendar, blocking out time to be alone so you can paint the kitchen cabinets, write a poem, read Tolstoy, cook, sew, exercise, or just "be." Treat these planned occasions as "meetings" and use them to make yourself unavailable to other people's manipulations. "I have a meeting," or "I'm sorry, I have a conflict" are acceptable ways of saying "no." If you are at the constant mercy of other people's schedules and needs, you will become fragmented, disoriented, and unhappy.

■ *Reward yourself when you accomplish your goal.*
The late Bishop Fulton J. Sheen preached a sermon advising "first the famine, then the feast." After working hard under the pressure of a deadline, treat yourself to dinner at a favorite restaurant. Make an appointment for a pampering massage. You are more likely to face a challenge with equanimity when you plan a reward to follow.

■ *Work smarter, not harder.*
Tackle the most difficult tasks during the part of the day when you feel most refreshed. Use the time when you don't have that creative edge to putter, file, or prepare new projects for a better time. Quit while you are ahead, and come back refreshed.

■ *Go to bed one hour earlier.*
Waking up an hour before you must, to the quiet of the morning, will give you a jump on the day, and that one peaceful hour spent alone can be worth more than three hours fractured with interruptions later on. You *will* feel better after you think through the day ahead.

■ *Be in training for life.*
Exercise makes you feel better and gives you energy. Dance, jog, walk, play a sport, swim. Move all the parts that can move. Regularly. Treat your brain as you would a muscle: it requires exercise also. Read Emerson, Yeats, Marcus Aurelius, Socrates,

Quit while you're ahead!

Plato, or Dickinson before going to sleep; then concentrate on their wisdom as you get ready to start work the following day.

■ *Create a positive image of the day.*

New research affirms the real power of positive thinking and tells us that optimists handle stress better than pessimists do. Cancer therapist Dr. Cowles says: "We all face some form of negative emotion on a daily basis. And, it has been well documented that the repeated negative emotions such as anger, frustration, unfulfillment, denial, depression or tension can affect our immune response in an adverse manner. We have the potential for small negatives to become small illness or something more serious. We must counteract those negatives by caring for ourselves to make certain that such emotions as joy, satisfaction, laughter, love and feelings of self-worth are experienced too. And it's their positive emotion boosters that offset the negative. We need to develop the habit of being good to ourselves so that those actions become our system of checks and balances for our mind/body interaction. The truth is we can never outdo being good and caring for ourselves. And the reason is, there is simply too much of life to deal with and push through. I never hear someone say, 'I've been feeling too good. I need a few bad days.' No, the truth is we constantly deplete our energy and we need to replenish it on a daily basis with self-nourishing experiences. Being good to oneself is not selfish, it is self-preserving."

Hold high expectations for your day. Cultivate your vitality. Persevere. The effort you make now will benefit you tomorrow. By stretching yourself and giving your all *today*, you will surprise yourself by how much you can achieve tomorrow. Take risks in new areas. Success is attained only through a series of steps carefully and creatively begun and guided to a high standard of excellence. Today is going to be *your* day.

■ *Don't want it all.*

Define what you really want—what you value—and have your actions follow your goals. Enjoy the process of all your activities. Make your pleasure factor a high priority. Learn how much you can handle and move forward with confidence. When you're accomplishing your personal goals you handle stress better because you glimpse the essence of things. Take time to feel the awe of life as you move through your day.

Two successful middle-aged divorced people in the advertising business met and fell in love in California. They worked for competing agencies but helped each other develop ideas and there was no jealousy on Philip's part that Gwen earned a little more money than he did. They loved to water-ski together and she enjoyed cooking for Philip, who was overweight: She taught him about carbohydrates, whole grains, roughage, and herbs in place of salty spices. Philip's weight dropped a little and his energy increased.

2.
HEALTH

They began talking about marriage and Gwen said she'd consider marrying him on one condition: That they would go to a health spa together on their honeymoon where knowledgeable doctors could put them both on a good healthful regimen. At first Philip refused. He wanted to go to Paris and show Gwen around, and eat in the best restaurants. She'd never been outside the United States and was tempted. But because Philip admittedly abused his health with bad eating habits—too much fried food—he listened carefully and agreed to get their life off to a healthy start.

They could always go to Paris after they'd established healthful ground rules so that a normal cholesterol level, blood pressure, and weight could be maintained. Gwen loved Philip and had no interest in becoming a widow. They began their marriage paying attention to the well-being of their own and each other's bodies.

Years ago I remember asking my husband at the breakfast table if he thought he'd like chicken for dinner. I laugh now, but at the time I was hurt. "Please," he said. "I can't even think of chicken, I'm trying to enjoy my fried eggs."

3.
MENUS

Years ago I wrote a series of menus for "couples on the run" for *Harper's Bazaar*. Plan meals well in advance—it brings order.

Decide ahead of time when you'll stay home for dinner and when you'll have a night off. Get together with your mate once a week and plan the whole week's dinner menus based on healthful, nutritious food. When you both make decisions about food you can take into consideration diets, fiber, cutting down on meat and fats. Both partners contribute to special seasonal requests—"Let's have peaches for dessert," or "Let's have nothing but corn on the cob, sliced tomatoes, and onions for dinner one night this week." This mutual planning session is fun and you both have a vote. By writing out the menu on a five-by-seven-inch file card and posting it each week in the kitchen, you both can remember not to have chicken for lunch Wednesday, knowing it's roast chicken night.

Menu planning is fun. Be playful in your inventions. Remember that chicken can be served a hundred ways. Save your menus in a pretty box (Il Papiro, the Italian paper company with three shops in New York, now features in their catalog an array of marbleized shoe boxes, a perfect size to hold your menu cards). I have a friend who writes out her menus on sensuous postcards of food and eating scenes. She places the pretty menu card on the table for beauty and to display the menu neatly written on the back. Stretch your imagination to have an abundant range of colorful menu selections. If you find you're stuck and need inspiration, flip through your past month's menus and repeat some of the more successful combinations, things you both liked.

No one should have to cook every night. At least one night have Lean Cuisine, Chinese food delivered, or delicacies you can pick up at a specialty food store. Specify what variety of pasta you want in your Lean Cuisine and look at the Chinese takeout list and specify which things you'll order. Put your favorites on labeled cards so you don't forget which kind of dish you like best. The more specific you are, the more you will zero in on the favorites you both enjoy. Because you both plan the menu, there won't be hurt feelings if a few of the experiments aren't successful.

Serve food on a platter so each of you can take the portion you want. Never get upset when someone doesn't clean his plate. Americans on the average are twenty pounds overweight. When we feel puffy we have to eat less.

Food is not love, but eating can be a loving occasion. Make a big effort to have a regular time when you sit down to dinner together. Samuel Johnson felt if you didn't dine well, the rest of your life was suspect. Not taking time to stop everything and share a lovely meal together is a new aberration. "Grazing" is anti-communication. Whether you eat at the kitchen table, the dining room, or in a restaurant, one of the greatest moments of the day is when you come together to eat while you enjoy the luxury of each other's undivided attention. By planning set menus together, you are setting priorities—dinner for two.

In her Personal Health column for the *New York Times*, Jane E. Brody wrote about changing unhealthful habits and one of her points was: "Adopting new ways of eating or managing stress is far more difficult than remembering to floss your teeth every day or buckle your seat belt. . . . Instilling new habits requires thought, deliberate action and sometimes temporary physical discomfort. But once they are adopted, you can feel just as comfortable with new habits as with the old."

Ms. Brody believes that a healthful habit "promotes feelings of self-confidence and control that carry over into other areas—work and interpersonal relationships—and it gives a sense of inner peace. It has been shown repeatedly, for example, that fit people tend to be more productive, more efficient and better organized. They get more done and have more fun doing it."

Delight in the moment.

4.
EXERCISE

Our weight fluctuates, one of us has a tricky back, one has arthritis, the other has a high cholesterol count. We're in the boat together. I am often asked, "When do you exercise?" This question amuses me because it is the one area of my life I can't get a firm grip on. In the morning I like to write before I go to the office. In the evening I like to stay late at the office, and now that our daughters are in college I have the luxury of time. We often have plans in the evenings. When is it convenient to work up a sweat?

The answer is never, yet my life depends on my staying energetic. Regular exercise helps the way I look, feel, and act. I make exercise a priority and do it automatically, two mornings a week, without excuses. I've tried to exercise more and can't maintain my schedule, so I've made an agreement with myself to exercise two early mornings and if I can, I squeeze in a late Saturday morning class before going out to lunch with Peter, which is a Saturday ritual.

Tuesday and Thursday mornings I get up an hour earlier, have my juice and coffee, write in my journal, write a few letters, and attempt to do some writing before I exercise. In this way I don't have to give up my morning writing. After I exercise I always feel full of energy, ready to hit the day feeling good and good about myself.

Your body will get accustomed to the amount of exercise it gets, so consistency is important. Don't fall into the tendency of sabotaging your own success and happiness. Your self-esteem and image depend on your ability to schedule regular exercise. I don't have the discipline to exercise alone so I have someone I exercise with: you can too. Make it a priority: set a time, make a date, play music, and get moving.

5. DRESS CODE AT HOME

A man who wanders around the house in only his underdrawers insults his wife and children. One man loved to wear the same old blue shirt every evening at home. "I wish I had three just like this one," he told his partner with a purr. Frustrated, she said, "It's okay for you, but do you have any idea how boring it is for me? I see you drag out the same old shirt night after night and I sense the kind of evening we'll have, and I sense it'll be a drag." A man wandering around the house in pajamas that aren't buttoned at the fly isn't sexy. A soiled bathrobe with no sash is sloppy.

In our apartment the house rule is: We can wear anything we want in our bedrooms. However, when we are in the rest of the apartment we are dressed appropriately to receive friends of our spouse or our children. Since we encourage our family to come and go with friends in the apartment, we try to look decent.

The secret is that we enjoy coming home from work and bathing, changing into fresh clothes. Dressing for dinner tends to wipe away the stresses of the day and creates an attractive climate for a nice evening together. Dress in fresh clothes every evening, not just when you go out. It's fun if you hold up a choice of two shirts to your mate. "Which one tonight?" Variety does spice things up. Be sure you don't fall into "the uniform" mentality in which you wear the same style and color nightgown or pajama every evening at bedtime. The first and last impressions each day are important. If you feel your mate's bedtime clothes could stand a lift, buy him an elegant robe or for her, a peignor. What a loving and subtle act, which will give you both equal hours of pleasure! Watch out for padding around in funny old slippers. They might be comfortable, but they are more appropriate in a nursing home.

Wrap yourself in your essence.

When you live with someone, approximately half the time you spend together you are sleeping. It is rare when two people have the same sleep patterns over an extended period of time. A friend, for instance, needed a great deal more sleep the first several weeks after he quit smoking. A doctor I respect advised me that most healthy adults can manage well on five and a half to six hours of sleep per night. Pressure, stress, pain, mood, alcohol, and attitude obviously affect how well anyone actually sleeps in that time period.

6.
SLEEP
REQUIREMENTS

When you share a bedroom with your mate, the person wanting the most sleep deserves to have the room dark and quiet. The smallest noises can become enormous irritations to someone in need of rest. The more tired we are, the more intense sounds become. To the tired mate trying to sleep, it can be extremely annoying for someone to be reading the newspaper and ripping out articles to save. Bright lamplight can be distracting too. Allow the one who needs to rest to have the room to himself. This way it will be there for you also, when you are tired and in need of sleep.

Announce ahead of time when you intend to go to bed so it won't be an inconvenience to the one who wishes to stay up later. The same rule should apply for waking up. If one of you has to get up early and the other is able to sleep in, it is a kindness to have all your clothes organized the night before so you make a minimum of noise and disturbance in the morning. Once awake, it is hard for some of us to get back to sleep. If you have a cold and a bad cough, it is thoughtful to offer to sleep in another room. This way you won't pass on the germs, and the healthy person doesn't look mean having to kick you out of the bed.

A bed that is shared by two people has to support two backs. Often one person finds the mattress comfortable and the other suffers. If either of you has any kind of a tricky back it is best to solve the back problem by putting a board under the mattress on the side of the one with the trick back or have two separate mattresses so each person can have what he requires in the way of firmness. A man weighing thirty to fifty pounds more than his wife pushes the mattress down, leaving little support for the lighter-weight spouse. If you want a sixty-inch-wide queen-size bed, you can have two thirty-inch mattresses specially made.

The most important thing is to awaken refreshed. When I feel a bit dragged down I go to bed one hour earlier for a week and the results are amazing. I wake up before the alarm clock goes off, ready to hit the new day. Try it. If you find you are still feeling tired, not waking up feeling rested, you may need more sleep. Early evening sleep is the best.

Some find naps refreshing, others don't. My friend Cathy is a cheerful soul who has tried to take a Sunday afternoon nap with her husband Bill while the baby sleeps. "I can't risk it," she laughs. "I always wake up grumpy, wondering where the other six hours are. Naps are not for me." Do what feels best for you, but get the sleep you need.

"If at first you don't succeed, try, try again."
—*WILLIAM EDWARD HICKSON*

This magical room with running water is a place for rejuvenation—a place to go to pamper, cleanse, shower or bathe, and prepare ourselves for the day, the evening, or bed. It can also be a place where a busy couple can meet and talk as they perform their individual ablutions.

Usually in the privacy of our own bathrooms, we attend to necessary maintenance. When you invite your mate into the bathroom, be sure you are performing a sensuous act; be enjoying an extravagantly lavish soak in the tub. Don't be clipping your toenails. A little mystery is important.

I shared a bathroom with my sister and two brothers growing up, so sharing a bathroom with Peter, who is relatively neat, seems a luxury by comparison. However, he takes twenty minutes in the bathroom each morning and when we're both leaving for the office at the same time, it causes me to become anxious when I have to rush.

Monday, Wednesday, and Friday mornings I get up earlier than Peter and luxuriate in the bath ritual, taking my time, washing my hair, blow-drying it, and using electric curlers. I'm first in the bathroom those three weekday mornings. Tuesday and Thursday mornings I exercise first and use the bathroom after Peter has finished.

Build in enough time to spend a few minutes straightening up the bathroom for your partner. Wipe out the sink, check to be sure there is plenty of toilet paper, fold the towels and hang them up. Wipe off the counter and mirror. Have designated towel bars for you and your partner so your wet towels won't be reused by mistake. Be sure the floor isn't wet. My mother was strict raising her four children and made us walk out of the bathroom backward, checking to be sure everything was neat. Pay attention and try to have the bathroom clean and neat for your partner.

Have a specific concealed place for your necessities, and another for your mate's grooming needs. You need one additional storage area for mutual shared supplies. When I design medicine cabinets for clients I have the right- and left-hand wings for each person's

7.
SHARING A
BATHROOM

117

separate essentials and a third area, a cabinet or cupboard, for the extra supplies both people use.

In front of the window in our bathroom I have a Victorian wicker sewing stand I use for all my makeup. The walls surrounding the window are mirrored, so in the morning I have good natural light which helps me see to make up. Everything is in one place for this. Next to the tub, we have a pastel flower-decorated basket with shampoos, conditioners, soaps, sponges, face mitts, bath oils, gels, and bubbles, so once we're in the bath we have everything at hand.

The only thing we need near the sink is toothpaste, tooth-brushes, and dental floss and I keep them in a polished silver baby cup in a nearby cupboard. I love silver and keep silver polish in with my other supplies in the bathroom because we have pretty bottles with silver tops there that need care. We never keep any functional items such as toothbrushes, razors, toothpaste, tampons, or deodorant visible. Our mouthwashes, green Scope and red La-voris, are in attractive cut crystal decanters adding color to our green-tiled countertop.

Next to the toilet we have a wicker rack for magazines with the latest *Art & Antiques, Gourmet, The Economist, M, W, McCall's, House Beautiful* and *HG*.

Never leave your bath ritual in a rush. Make the preparation for your partner part of the pleasure of your ceremony, anticipating his or her rejuvenation from the time spent there. There are hundreds of little ways to express love and caring. Make the most of the subtle. The bathroom can be a soothing place to retreat to, day or night, when two caring people make a little extra effort to experience grace in this special room with running water.

8. NOISES

A lot of harmony is essential when people live together. This requires synchronization of noises, tuning in to the same radio station and fitting in well. One evening I came home from work and felt attacked by sounds—the Iran-Contra hearing was on tele-vision, and different music blasted from two bedrooms. I walked into our bedroom to escape into the soothing sounds of Lite FM and our radio station had been reset to a Spanish-speaking station by the cleaning woman. Noises have the power to enrich our lives at home or set our teeth on edge.

Having the apartment quiet enough so we can hear the church bells across the street is soothing. Listening to birds sing, going to the window and listening to a heavy rainfall—we can appreciate these noises because they are natural and spontaneous. Listening to some favorite classical music or reminiscing while listening to Frank Sinatra adds a dimension of pleasure to the atmosphere. What often happens, however, when we live together, is that sounds get out of sync and what has the potential to soothe and delight can cause irritation and frustration. It's all a matter of communicating mood and desires. Close doors to isolate conflicting sounds. Television can be an irritating distraction to those not watching. For some, earphones help; for others, the solution may be a closed door.

It's always nice to keep in mind your mate's needs. If the urge hits you for some really loud rock music, a Walkman could satisfy your desires and not drive your mate crazy. When you live together, space is always restricted and sounds travel. Be aware that what you do in one room often affects others in a room nearby. Someone going to the kitchen to get a drink—cracking ice on the countertop, slamming the cupboard doors—sounds a lot more violent to the person not participating in the activity.

Try to minimize negative sounds: close a door gently, remember if someone is sleeping and tiptoe. After a tough day at work our nerves tend to be a bit frayed, we're tired, and we might have a slight headache. Embrace quiet so that there is a sense of calm and tranquillity at home.

If a drawer makes a horrible noise, oil it. If a fan is noisy, get it fixed. When you order a new kitchen stove hood fan, listen to it for a few minutes in the store before you have it installed and discover it is too noisy. If you live in a crowded area and the street noises keep you from sleeping well, investigate Thermopane windows. When you put away pots and pans, glide them into place—

don't be a bull when you unstack the dishwasher. If you are going to hang a painting and plan to use a hammer, announce this beforehand so no one will be startled.

9.
VOICE
TONES

Through the sound of our words, the tone of our voices, we sing different tunes, creating music or cacophony. We hold great power to communicate tenderness and love through our choice of words and how we voice them. A lovely muted voice is soothing and easy on the ear of the listener, like a Brahms concert. The more wound-up I am, the more my voice magnifies. We all should concentrate on listening to our own voice and how we project.

Eudora Welty wrote lovingly of her parents' love for each other in her touching book *One Writer's Beginnings*. She described her memory of her mother being downstairs cooking while her father was upstairs; they would be whistling a duet together.

Listen to the voices of those you admire. Slow down your speech—this helps you to speak in a gentle tone of voice. Be aware of your breathing. By taking several deep breaths you calm yourself.

Sound as beautiful as you are.

10.
INTERRUP-
TIONS

"Do you want me to read you what René Dubos says about our biological nature?" inquires Peter in a friendly, sharing way. Of course I want to hear, but when I'm in the middle of writing a sentence I can't stop even to answer his question until I put a period at the end of my thought. Peter was just being loving, sharing an insight.

There are times to interrupt and times not to be interrupted. Only you know the difference. You may be reading, paying the bills, or writing a letter, and your mate obviously wants to be with you and tries in sweet ways to capture your attention. This can be adorable in moments when you are not in the flow of something important. Be spontaneous and put down what you are doing and answer, "Please tell me." Whether this break lasts for a moment, five minutes, or three hours, the spontaneity will lead to serendipity, and you have to let go enough to notice and be open to the closeness of that moment. Catch these little interruptions as moments of affection and run with them.

Be kind. Everyone is struggling.

The Buddhist philosophy of being here now means letting go of attachment. We're always doing something, but that doesn't mean we're not game to do something else if invited! I'll always find ways to entertain myself, but usually I'd prefer to have someone I love share something with me, whether it's a joke, a quote, a story, a kiss, or a bike ride. Be open. Welcome interruptions. If your partner jumps up and says, "Let's go to the four o'clock showing of *A Room with a View*; I'm in the mood," go. Have fun; you may end up having an early supper out. Break the routine of planning everything ahead of time. Tell your mate when you want to be left alone undisturbed and for approximately how long. When you do, it allows your partner to dream up fun things to do when you are free. This way there won't be any hurt feelings or misunderstandings. Usually you both can sense the other's mood. Let your intuition guide you.

Most often Peter and I can be together in the same room even in those key times when we can't be interrupted. It is not always necessary to go to another room and close the door if you express your wish not to be disturbed. If someone forgets, it is usually followed by a quick apology and a smile.

Try never to interrupt someone's train of thought by anticipating the end of their sentence. If they pause for air, you shouldn't complete their thought for them. Give your mate unhurried time to express his or her thoughts. When a mate chimes in, "Yes, yes. What is your point?" or, "Get on with it," this chills self-expression and spontaneous communication. Listen and don't criticize. Something meaningful might need to be expressed. I've discovered I become frustrated by these mild interruptions only if I am in a grumpy mood and in that case I excuse myself and go to a private room where I can recover. This seems to work out well for us and makes for contentment.

11.
"MAY I HELP?"

Gentleness is always
loving.

Offer your help around the house without being asked. Sometimes it's obvious when help would be appreciated. Throw out the old newspapers, get a new roll of toilet paper and put it in the holder, change a burned-out light bulb, water and mist the plants, bring the dry cleaning into the bedroom, or plump up the sofa pillows. You both share in the advantages of an attractive, well-ordered household and you both have to pitch in on its upkeep. It is nice to offer to help with the necessary chores without someone having to sound demanding or nagging by always having to ask you for help.

One of the most frustrating moments for all of us is when we sit down comfortably ready to read the paper or a book and just as we feel the luxury of a moment's peace, we hear "Could you please come and help me?" It's far better to offer to do an errand or two, and then announce you're going to do some reading. If the answer to your offer to help is "No, thank you," you're off the hook, guilt-free, no matter how much the rest of the household bustles about.

If you really want to do some reading or puttering and your mate is busy moving about the house or apartment, it is best to say you'd love to do the dishes tonight because now you're busy with a project. This balances the scale and the one working knows he'll have his turn to relax later. Before you sit down to do your project ask, "Is there anything I can bring you?" This kindness shows courtesy and reminds the other person he is appreciated.

12.
"I'M SORRY"

When we do something we regret and we are sincerely sorry, say "I'm sorry." It can ease the pain for the other person. Saying "I'm sorry" at certain moments shows sensitivity and caring.

Last spring I was in London with Peter and we received an urgent phone message to call one of his clients. I had a bad cold and was feeling a bit testy from jet lag. Later on that week, I was to give the commencement address where I went to boarding school in Massachusetts and I was concerned about doing a good job. I had periodically read over my talk and had mild anxiety attacks.

I've trained myself not to use notes when I lecture but usually I talk about design and I have colorful slides to accompany my spontaneous remarks. Here I'd have fifty-four excited, emotional graduates, their parents, family, faculty, and friends. There would be no slides to lean on to jog my memory. It was rather frightening and frankly I was nervous.

I had asked Peter months ahead if he would come to lend moral support and he had accepted, saying, "I wouldn't miss it for anything." He was looking forward to being there for the exciting event. It's not every day I get to go back to my school and talk to the graduating class about their future. I was excited and wanted him there.

The emergency with his client meant that he had to leave New York at the crack of dawn Saturday in order to be in Taiwan for a meeting on Monday. Saturday I was giving the talk in Massachusetts. I smelled a rat as I sipped my breakfast coffee and eavesdropped on his important phone call. My poached eggs were runny and by now cold. I had a sinking spell. "What's the emergency, darling?"

"I'm leaving for Taiwan Saturday morning. How's the coffee?"

If only he had come over to me, given me a little kiss or a pat and said, "I'm sorry." But when we are really upset, the obvious eludes us. I knew in my gut he was sorry, this situation was beyond his control, but I couldn't help feeling sorry for myself which I hate to do.

Finally it all worked out: my daughter Alexandra came to Massachusetts and brought a dear friend along for company and we had a lot of fun. Peter later apologized. What we learned is that when "I'm sorry" is said *immediately* it has enormous power. Unnecessary anguish is eliminated.

Try to feel the other person's pain or discomfort and ease it by telling them you care. The late historian and author of *Civilization*, Sir Kenneth Clark, said, "I believe in courtesy, the ritual by which we avoid hurting people's feelings by satisfying our own egos."

13.
"PLEASE"

When someone asks me to do something beginning with "please," I melt. Please is the entering wedge, a courteous way to begin a request. When "please" precedes "move your chair" it is less an order and more a request. It is impossible to say "please" in an angry, hostile way. So when you compose a request, "please" sets the tone. "Please don't buy a new camera" expresses an opinion. "Don't buy a new camera" implies an order.

Say "please" and soften the atmosphere around you. "Please empty the garbage." "Please wear your red tie with blue polka dots." "Please exercise with me." "Please come with me to the drugstore." There is magic in "please"—a nonhostile, gracious word that helps you get your way nicely so you and the other person are both pleased. Please?

14.
"THANKS"

The more secure we are inside ourselves, the more likely we are to express gratitude toward others. I was at a client's breakfast table years ago and we were discussing the lovely dinner party we'd been to the night before. The husband said he was going to write a little thank-you note and the wife interrupted. "Don't. They were lucky to have us there. It looks as though you're groveling to write them a thank-you note." As three young children listened, the husband gently said, "I'll write a note for both of us. It's courteous and thoughtful." The children's and my eyes went from the mother to the father and the unspoken consensus was that the father was 100 percent right.

When we live together there are nitty-gritty everyday things that have to be done to maintain order and the smooth operation of a household. Just because the divison of labor may relegate meal preparation to one person and clean-up duty to the other, a quick recognition of gratitude can certainly lighten the load and make you feel glad to have made the effort. We all are soothed by recognition.

Thanks must be sincere. If someone is having an off day and dinner is served in a lackluster way with no apparent effort to make a special moment—be helpful, clean up, tomorrow will be better.

Where your senses are awakened and the atmosphere is made extremely pleasant because of a little extra attempt, I would rush to thank that person. Honesty gives "thanks" its meaning.

Once I leave the apartment in the morning I don't get to a full-length mirror again until I undress in the evening. I pull out a compact and freshen up my lipstick and powder my nose a few times during the day. It's invariably after the compact is put away that some lipstick ends up on my front teeth. I want to be told. If I have a flake of dandruff at my hairline I'd hope my mate would flick it away. The same with spinach or pepper lodged between my teeth. I want to be told. It's not heckling, it shows you care.

If you discover your wife has a run in her stocking and you tell her before she leaves the house, that is a kindness. If there's a spot on your husband's tie and you see it while he is dressing, tell him. If, however, you notice your wife's run on the bus just before she is going to have an important job interview, don't say anything. There is no way she can get to a store to buy a spare pair of stockings and still be on time for the interview. Her confidence would probably be shattered and she would feel anxious.

Timing is everything. You shouldn't look at your spouse's necktie at a restaurant and comment, "Your tie is full of soup." Remember how fragile we all are. Be tender.

Standing at the front door of their house waiting for the baby-sitter to come up the path, Ellen glanced at her lovely garden and then at her husband, her eye casing him up and down: "Russell looked awful. Here I'd gone out and bought a new dress. It was our anniversary and we were going back to the restaurant where he proposed nine years ago. He runs a small publishing house and gets carried away with his work. At the office he takes his jacket off and rolls up his sleeves. Can you imagine, on our anniversary he came home late? He didn't even change his clothes or bathe! I was furious." She didn't let it ruin the evening, however. He did have a beautiful gold pin, which he'd thoughtfully had engraved,

15.
TIMING
IS EVERYTHING

16.
DRESS CODE
AWAY FROM
HOME

Contentment comes from appreciation, not wealth.

which he presented to her as a complete surprise at the restaurant.

Now, when there are special events in the evenings, she calls Russell at the office in plenty of time for him to come home and change before going out. We all need to be reminded to make the little extra effort and both mates feel so much better.

A successful businesswoman was being sent to Paris for a series of meetings and she invited her boyfriend to join her for a week, staying at the Ritz. Edith loves clothes and planned her wardrobe with great care, not only anticipating what she'd wear for her meetings but what she'd wear in her free evenings with Gerry. She mapped out an attractive wardrobe for her entire stay, coordinating her accessories so that the colors went well together and had some style and dash. After all, this was to be Paris and the Ritz.

The first evening Edith and Gerry arrived, they decided to rest and to have an early dinner right there at the Ritz, a luxury many of us know only in our dreams. As they were leaving their hotel room Edith noticed something incongruous—Gerry had on a pair of running sneakers. Trying not to explode, she inquired, "Why would you consider coming to Paris, staying at the Ritz, and wearing sneakers?" They weren't going jogging, they were going out to dine in one of the world's finest and most elegant restaurants. Sneakers! Not only did Gerry have on sneakers, his necktie was dark and dreary. Funereal. When she pleaded with him please to wear a more exciting tie and to change out of his running shoes, Gerry confessed he had forgotten to pack neckties and shoes! He always wears sneakers on airplanes.

They fought. He became defensive. "You're too clothes-conscious, you're too superficial, too concerned with appearances." She argued back, "You are being treated to a week in Paris, staying at one of the most romantic hotels in the world, and you don't even care what you pack. And I'm stuck with you. I can't stand it. What's wrong with you?"

At dinner Edith was determined to enjoy her asparagus and grilled sole, which she'd anticipated to the point of near fixation, and she tried to blank the rage from her mind. They had some wine, Edith loosened up a bit, and they ended up having a pleasant evening in spite of the beginning. Edith convinced herself that the waiters and guests weren't staring at her mate's sneakers and that the drab tie looked better by candlelight.

In the morning they went shopping, taking full advantage of being in Paris, and outfitted Gerry—snappy shoes with tassels, a double-breasted blazer with gold buttons, and three lively, colorful silk ties.

It embarrasses a woman to go to a restaurant with her date and be told at the door that he needs a tie and jacket. Surely a man's own jacket from his closet looks better than the baggy, wrinkled jacket and idiotic tie the restaurant lends to guests.

Busy people make dates and decide where to meet; because of logistics the place may be an awkward one to be kept waiting, like a garage, a busy street corner, or a lobby. When you keep your spouse waiting it sends out signals that his or her time doesn't matter. "Let her wait; she knows I'll show up." Immediately, when we are kept waiting, we worry that we got our signals crossed. Often there is a conversation back and forth until the place is agreed on. When kept waiting you are filled with doubt. Has something happened? Am I in the right place?

It is not worth causing this stress to your mate just because you wanted to make a few phone calls or clear your desk. Plan to be a few minutes early, rather than cutting it too close. That way you can anticipate the arrival—you can watch for that reassuring smile; it can be a pleasant moment of expectation. When someone is afraid, their tension shows in their voice. "Where were you?" shouted in an anxiety-ridden voice by someone who has been kept waiting could start a fight. "Where do you think I was?" the late arriver defensively shouts back. This scenario is avoidable. Take a few extra minutes to assure thoughtfulness. If you and your mate establish mutual punctuality, you will have reason to be concerned if you are kept waiting—it *will* be for an unavoidable reason, which you'll easily be able to respect. Everyone values their own time

17.
BEING
DEPENDABLE

127

and when you safeguard another's time, it is a way of expressing your respect, even affection. You be the first one there. Be calm, collected, and smiling.

18.
PAY
ATTENTION

Value all experiences.

There are times when we long for the undivided attention of our partner. But when people are together a great deal, it is impossible to pay attention to the other person 100 percent of the time. People living together need freedom and space to move around and pursue their own interests. With really close rapport, two people can be together silently and still communicate. There are certain times that should be allocated so both partners can give the other their undivided attention.

Make moments when you can drop everything and be together without interruption. Pay attention. A good time to do this is right after work when you get home, so you can set the stage for the evening. Talk things over. Listen carefully. Encourage your mate to say what's on his or her mind. Be patient. Let there be pauses. Don't interrupt. Be attentive to the silences. Ask thoughtful questions.

If you have had something important happen to you during the day, let your mate know you want to talk things over. The telephone should not interfere during these special moments together when you both are opening up in the privacy and security of your home. If you don't have an answering machine, take the phone off the hook or let it ring if there isn't anyone else at home who can answer it for you. When someone is in the middle of a thought, once it is interrupted it is hard to get back to that same thread and the spell is broken.

Sam, a "Type A" businessman, loves to take his wife out to dinner now that the children have grown up and left home. Marsha doesn't have a job, and while she occupies herself during the day doing church work and visiting the elderly shut-ins from her parish, she is starved for his company. Invariably Sam fidgets, looks around everywhere but at his adoring wife, strikes up a conversation with the neighboring tables and the waitress, and when he isn't doing the talking he eavesdrops on the conversations around him.

Marsha is so glad to get out of the house she puts up with it but it bothers her. People don't have to fight to be unkind or irritating to each other. Not being attentive can hurt just as badly as screaming or having a fistfight. Pay attention to how you treat others. A good way to concentrate on another person is to look into their eyes. Not only will this focus your attention, it signals to the other person that your attention is undivided.

When you live with someone, there is no avoiding the unpleasant aspects inevitable in all relationships. When you're struggling through a difficult period, often you feel it will never end. I have a friend who was hospitalized for five months during her first pregnancy. It was equally hard on both partners and impatience never helps. Awful, painful things happen to nice people and when we are patient, and understand the problems, we can work through them. This deepens our relationship and we are better able to face the next problem.

**19.
PATIENCE**

It's relatively easy to be cheerful when everything is going well. It's when things get rough that cheerfulness is a challenge. Each person has to be a good sport and muster enough reserve strength of character to help the other. Often it is harder to be the person living with someone who is ill than to be the patient. As awful as something appears today, patience will lessen your discouragement. When one door is closed to you, another might open the way to living in more abundance. You will both emerge different people and the patience you demonstrate during the crisis is love in action. Patience will reward you in mysterious ways. Learn the capacity of enduring hardship or inconvenience without complaint. You will always be the winner.

When someone you live with confides in you something terribly important, don't judge what you hear. Be patient, listen, and show unqualified love. Ask short questions that open up more doors to the facts. The truth is the prize. Once you fully understand what

Quietly listen.

you have to deal with, you can help become part of the solution. A successful actor confided in his wife, "I drink too much, it's affecting my work and I want to do something about it." She hugged him nervously and said, "Oh no you don't, you're just tired." She should have asked what she could do to help. You won't always hear what you want to hear: try to hear the truth, try to help. If someone confides she's pregnant don't say, "You couldn't be." Instead, ask how she feels about being pregnant. You may be horrified, but she could be tickled pink! Don't judge.

20.
TOLERANCE

Understand that none of us is perfect. We have to remember the Old Testament: "With all thy getting, get understanding." There has to be a certain degree of putting up with someone else's behavior, allowing leeway for variation from your own standards. Respect the nature of the other person and grow to tolerate your differences.

Tolerance is a cushion, allowing you to move ahead in peace, putting up with things that you have no control over and enduring life during times of hardship or pain.

When someone is basically good and you are living together, there are so many optimistic things you can focus on. Dwell on these. Constantly riding herd, picking at every move takes time and energy away from the important thing—living beautifully together. Remember kindness: it usually leads to tolerance. Tolerance pays big dividends when you live together.

When the delegates signed the Constitution in Philadelphia two hundred years ago, the Preamble read "to form a more prefect Union"—not a perfect union. This tolerance gave greater assurance to the country's prosperity and freedom. Tolerance is the key to opening doors to happier personal relationships.

- Make love pacts: make a date always for the same day of the week and keep it.

- Have a dream box: clip pictures of things you both love: a painting, vacation spots, a house.

- Bring life to the heart of your home. Have a flowering plant on your kitchen table for daily appreciation and wonder.

- Keep a special note from your mate in your wallet or desk drawer and sneak a peek to get you through the day.

- Call your spouse at work and inquire how his day is coming along.

- Hold hands when you walk together, give him little pinches or kisses to keep him smiling.

- Try to think of something positive to say to your mate. By letting others know you notice and appreciate, you reinforce and give encouragement.

- Install a small music system in your kitchen so you can enjoy beautiful music together while cooking and eating simple attractive dinners for two. Store some tapes in a drawer and let your mate pick a favorite tape.

- Praise a thoughtful act.

- Be a good listener.

- Say grace together.

- Inquire whether your partner wants a back rub.

- Read a book about his favorite sport so you can share in his enthusiasm.

- Never forget to say I love you before going to bed.

- Never go to bed mad at each other.

- Invite your mate on your next business trip.

- Compose a poem or write a love letter and leave it for your mate.

- Sit down together and each make a "sensuous list." List all the physical things you can do for each other. Post the list on your closet door.

- Read quietly together.

- Ask before opening a package or borrowing a sweater—everyone needs control over personal property.

- Polish your mate's shoes as a surprise gesture of love.

- Have a picnic basket handy to pack with fresh food so that you can be spontaneous.

- Remember that any action involves the two of you and not just one.

- Be flexible.

- Offer your love a cup of tea for two at an unexpected time.

- Make a Saturday morning ritual of staying in bed together reading newspapers, magazines, and settling into a good book. Sip coffee and fresh-squeezed fruit juice. Turn off the telephone and listen to Frank Sinatra.

- Send your mate a flowering plant to his office with a love note.

- Surprise your partner and pick him up from work or meet him at the train station.

- Tell each other your dreams and fantasies.

- Don't be afraid to say "I love you" in front of others.

- Take turns being the star: let him shine at his office party.

- Put potpourri in a small antique box and keep the lid open.

- Call if you are working late or bringing home unexpected guests.

- Be considerate of your mate's need to stay in touch with his family.

- Give your mate a book you particularly enjoyed.

- On Valentine's Day, send *him* flowers. Buy *him* red-and-white-striped pajamas.

- Blow up a romantic picture of the two of you, frame it, and hang it in a spot for everyone to see.

- Surprise her with breakfast in bed; maybe she will return the favor.

- Go clothes-shopping with your mate. Someone who really loves you will help you select the most flattering styles.

- Throw a dinner party and share in the planning, shopping, and cooking.

- Visit his alma mater and walk through his memories; those stories you keep hearing will have more meaning for you.

- When your mate is on a long business trip, send mail to the hotel: there is nothing like getting mail.

- Keep love letters tied together in ribbon and go through them when things seem to be going badly. Frame your favorite and hang it over your bed for both of you to enjoy.

- Make friends together with other couples with similar interests.

- Make a birthday special: make a fuss, start the day with a special breakfast in bed; continue the festivities all day.

- When he is sick, leave him a survival kit: his favorite magazines, books, remote control for the TV, soup, juices, and a handmade "feel better" card.

- Have a classical scholar teach you both Greek history before you take your dream trip to the Greek islands.

- Try not to raise your voice, even in the worst of fights.

- Split the chores, and do together things you both really hate; it's less of a drag with company.

- Start a project together: paint a room, refinish a flea-market find.

- Buy two Sunday papers; no fighting over the Magazine and the Book Review.

- Plan your weekend "escape at home" today.

- Set a schedule to allow enough time for each of you in the bathroom.

- Have two lamps by the bed, so you can read when you want and not disturb your mate.

- Take up chess together.

- When a crisis phone call comes, stand by, hold your love, and listen.

- Begin each day with a smile and a "good morning" to each other.

- Exercise together—at home in the morning or at a local health club.

- Offer to draw your mate a bubble bath. Birch, apricot, or almond?

- When your partner is sad, be kind and remain optimistic, showing you believe in him.

- Have weigh-ins to shed unnecessary pounds. Keep a chart of your losses (or gains!).

- Lift your spirits by taking a course together: ballroom dancing, cooking, or painting.

- Check in with each other during the day to say "hello" and "I miss you."

- Take up some of the slack if your mate is involved in a big project at work. Have dinner warming in the oven or get the dry cleaning that he has not had the time to pick up.

- Each of you pick a sanctuary in your home. Choose your favorite chair and re-cover it and keep your favorite books close by. This is your spot to come to and relax all by yourself.

■ When your mate demands time alone, don't fret: use this time to do things you love and he hates: get together with your friends and chat over coffee or go shopping together.

■ Create a calm, intimate, romantic world. Always light a candle at dinner. It forces you to stop and appreciate being together.

YOUR
GRACE
NOTES

Part Three

ENJOYING
OTHERS

7

Children

When two healthy people fall in love and marry it is normal and natural to want to have children. Children are a gift, providing continuation of the family tree. We look at our spouse's baby pictures and fantasize what our children will look like, how they will inherit the best of our combined qualities.

Yet we are usually still so young and full of questions. We have little experience other than what our parents gave us through their example, yet our lives are different from theirs. We can't look backward for answers about tomorrow. The world we face is very different today. How will we be able to cope?

I can't think of any other experience in my life that can compare with the joy of having children. They are my commitment, my pride and joy, my pleasure. Birth control helps give us a choice about when to have our children. In my experience, the children who have the best chances for happiness and stability are those who were wanted and planned for.

I allow my intuition to guide me in all my decisions regarding my children. Think of your children (or child) as naturally flowing into your life and being carried steadily forward by you like fresh clear water in a stream. When I was pregnant with my second child,

137

I sat playing "angel" with Alexandra beside a beautiful flowing brook, a peaceful, loyal presence during our long afternoon picnic. When our second daughter was born we named her Brooke and she has been that clear, steady, sparkling stream in our lives.

Trust the natural process. You will continue to be yourself after you become a mother or a father. Your child will open you up to more beauty and love: a wanted child is a loved child, and love makes you instinctively know what to do.

ACCEPTANCE   When you say yes to having a child it means you are preparing to accept the inner beauty of your child. A child fresh from the womb has no faults. Love is pure, your child's feelings are honest. Babies may have little worldly experience, but they are powerfully intuitive. Don't let anyone tell you that your baby's smile is the passing of gas or that he or she can't see you when they stare at you. Trust your feelings that every sign of love is making a difference.

I grew in huge leaps after the birth of my first daughter. I felt the powerful energy of the universe, part of a grand mystery. Alexandra and I learned much about life together. Great beauty comes with accepting that your child is of you but not yours, that she or he has a full and unique spirit. You are given the privilege of influencing your children through thousands of small daily acts. It is in this way that you build their character and strength. This responsibility is nothing to fear. After bringing a child into the world you will become more aware each day of the power you hold in your arms.

UNQUALIFIED   A parent has an obligation to see the clear beauty of the newborn
LOVE   human being who is his child—never qualify your love. Make sure it is unconditional and continuous. Although my mother was a strict

disciplinarian, a day never passed when I didn't feel her deep and abiding love, her passion and her care.

One Christmas Eve, four-year-old Alexandra developed pneumonia and was rushed in a snowstorm to the hospital with a temperature of 107 degrees. The girls shared a room then, and soon Brooke developed infectious bronchitis. Nursing the girls back to health was emotionally exhausting, especially when we realized Alexandra could have died. Pale and tired, my sinuses infected, I accepted the invitation of friends in Antigua to join them for a week of recovery. "You're a wreck and you need to get back in shape so you can take care of your daughters," Susan said. The plan was that after I had a few days alone, the girls would also get to escape the winter solstice and come down for some sun, warmth, and fresh air.

During those first days in my solitary room at this island escape I looked over the color Polaroid pictures I'd taken on Christmas day of sheet-white little Alexandra in an oxygen tent. At times the sadness of separation and of sheer exhaustion nearly overwhelmed me. My husband, who had not been as strongly affected emotionally, stayed to take care of the girls in New York. At dinner one evening I met a man from Colorado who was in Antigua with his wife. I explained why I was alone, that my husband was taking care of our two young recuperating daughters and they would all be down to join me the end of the week. A sensitive, compassionate man, he was most sympathetic when I told him of the agony I'd felt witnessing my child's serious illness.

"I know what it's like. My wife and I have six daughters," he explained.

"Six daughters? How wonderful. Please tell me, how do you give enough love and attention to six daughters? I'm struggling with two."

He smiled proudly. "We've been very lucky. Every day I tell each daughter I love her. Each of my children has that love reinforced every single day and has since her birth. When I'm on a business trip I call home and speak to each girl, one at a time, ask

Look for the beauty within another spirit.

how their day has been, and I listen. I tell her I miss her and I love her. The girls know how much I love them and think of them. They know I care." He paused for a moment, thinking of this. "I try to treat each daughter like an only child. By having an individual relationship with each one, caring about her individual interests, each girl feels loved. The fact that we are eight happy people at home creates an energy and vitality that regenerates itself. We thrive on each other."

This was quite a lesson for me as a young mother. So simple. I love you. Three words a day times six, and all of this father's daughters got to thrive in an atmosphere of love.

ACCENT THE POSITIVE

I believe Rollo May is right that none of us ever feels enough love. Giving unqualified love provides the right climate, but we must also create rituals for exchanging and sharing love.

Why is it that parents, in their attempt to teach us everything we'll need to know in order to get along well in life, have a tendency to criticize nearly everything we do? The mother who tells us we don't fit the clothes when we go to try on dresses in a store is the same person who tells us years later that we lack self-confidence.

Sarah, a forty-eight-year-old mother of two, remarried and moved with her new husband and children into a lovely old rambling farmhouse outside Boston. Sarah's mother Henriette lives in Chicago, and is fiercely independent and going strong at seventy-nine years of age. When Henriette came to visit Sarah she managed to point out every area that needed work. "The living room could use a paint job." "Those stairs look terrible without a runner." She made endless criticisms instead of noticing all the work and care Sarah and David had already put into renovation. It is so obvious to any sensitive person that there is just so much money to spend on fixing up an old house.

Why do our parents expect us to be thin, smart, perfect, and rich? Is it because deep down inside, every parent feels their own

Daydreaming helps foster an aesthetic sensitivity.

shortcomings and wants to right the wrongs through their children? Children of any age learn more from parents reinforcing their strengths than from criticism of shortcomings. When a child is picked at all day long his emotions will soon be threadbare.

I read recently that most conversation tends to be negative. When we sit down with a child or friend we tend to discuss the problems of the world, or to discuss an acquaintance who is not present. We should make an effort to be part of the solution, thinking of ways we can help solve problems, and to notice the good things in life, talking about what we enjoy. Our children will imitate us.

Since what is bleak in life is already obvious, a conscious effort to point out the positive in every situation will make life look brighter. Communicate your enthusiasms to your child. Enjoy together the sunlight filtering through the trees, the smell of fresh air, the robin on the branch. Paint a vibrant picture of life for them.

If your children hear nothing but gloom and doom, showing that you feel hopeless and powerless in your life, they will not learn how to take responsibility for making their own lives beautiful, not to mention their world. After all, our world will soon be in our children's hands. It is now that we must show them how to fight for a glorious future.

Encourage your children to take risks, explore unknown areas of interest, and develop more curious minds. Stress the fun of learning and don't be reluctant to learn new things yourself, even from your children. Show them by example how they can continue to learn new things every day of their lives.

Be available. Children learn from observation.

When you praise your children you build their self-esteem. When your son or daughter takes initiative to do something worthwhile, make a big point to encourage the effort made. Just as it's more fun to score a point in basketball in front of a cheering crowd, a child will try something new just for the love of it when you reinforce those efforts and help build his confidence.

When you have to instruct a child, teach him in positive terms, emphasizing the constructive and graceful paths and using assuring, encouraging words. If your son makes a grammatical error while telling a story, don't correct him in front of others. You risk embarrassing and humiliating him. Put yourself in his place: Would you like to be cut down in the middle of a sentence to have a weak spot pointed out? At the right time there will be a way to instruct him in a loving, supportive way. When you embarrass someone you lose your power to instruct.

MAKE AN EFFORT

Life requires that we make an effort. This is the only secret to happiness: we must try our best. Draw on a blackboard in the kitchen: MEDIOCRITY IS DULL. Let your children learn the psychological satisfaction of completing a project. Something done well is an accomplishment that satisfies the human spirit. Each tiny detail is an opportunity for your children to put a personal stamp on a task and bring more organization to their surroundings.

Children tell me that when they go the extra step, add the extra flourish, it is exciting. Energy springs from a positive attitude. If your children use all their energy positively to improve things around them, they'll discover optimism and find pleasure in even the smallest tasks.

PARENTING

First and foremost, be yourself. Trust that the universe will take care of your child. Kahlil Gibran wrote in *The Prophet*: "Your children are not your children. They are the sons and daughters of Life's longing for itself. They come through you but not from you. And though they are with you they belong not to you." The best way for you to influence your child is to be energetic, alive and passionate. Most of all, don't worry. Children usually manage well as long as their parents are happy. Avoid the mistake many parents fall into by being needy and dependent on a child. Gibran instructs: "You can give them your love but not your thoughts, for they have their own thoughts. You may house their bodies but not their souls, for their souls dwell in the house of tomorrow, which you cannot visit, not even in your dreams. You may strive to be like them, but seek not to make them like you. For life goes not backward nor tarries with yesterday."

You have to be responsible for your own separate life and live it as fully and creatively as possible. Being a parent should not become a role to play in which you cater to a child's needs at the expense of your own. When parents attempt this, the marriage and the child suffer. The best answer is compromise: handle your lives simultaneously, so that everyone's needs are met.

Let your child thrive with you as an intelligent, engaged, and curious person. Give your child the opportunity to be proud of you. Remember there is a generation gap. Try to get inside your child's head and understand the freshness of his or her perception.

Loving is even greater than being loved.

Think of yourself as a source of energy and channel this toward your child. You want to provide the space, the climate and the opportunity for your child to grow up to be productive and find life an exciting adventure. Remember, a child is sensitive to your emotions all the time, looking up to you as model and teacher. Be as open and honest as possible. We all make tremendous sacrifices for the things that really matter to us—choosing to have a child and caring for your child is a beautiful privilege. Don't complain. You have what you wanted. Be grateful you have someone so meaningful to love and nurture. In tandem, continue to learn and grow as a way of living and loving. Give your child an image of how wonderful life can be for a grown-up.

There is only one way to do a good job being a parent—be a great human being. Try never to be a burden to your child. They need your love but not the guilt of your emptiness. Keep your life full to brimming and watch your child blossom.

Madeleine L'Engle wrote about parenting so wisely in *A Circle of Quiet*. "In our terror of becoming destructive mothers and fathers, we refuse to be parents at all. We abdicate parenthood and turn over our responsibilities to strangers; the Sunday school teacher will teach morality . . ." We as parents must persevere in raising our children according to our own values and convictions. Do not lose the opportunity you have to influence your children—if you let go of this responsibility you'll be leaving the job to your children's friends, their parents, school and television and movies, which is a dangerous mistake.

Sigmund Freud believed that the characteristics of each person's mind can be accounted for by early influences. When a child is born he or she inherits biological characteristics and much potential, but these traits will blossom only in the right environment. An individual is shaped by the way of life of the family; you create the setting for your child's development.

The mother of the mystic monk Thomas Merton wrote a letter to her art teacher in Paris when she was engaged to Merton's father just before World War I, telling him she had no wish to join the ranks of mediocre artists; she was more interested in interior decoration and design:

"It seems to me there is no more fascinating subject in the world than the influence of surroundings on human character. And to study character with a view to making its surroundings what they should be by means of certain decoration of houses—that is what I want to try to do."

When she was pregnant with "Tom" she read every manual on child care she could borrow. If surroundings were so influential on character, she was determined her child would have the right ones.

Our most beloved philosophers and advisers have much to say about the importance of environment in a child's life. The late René Dubos believed "Homo sapiens are not born with the attributes essential for a truly human life but rather with potentialities that enable them to become human . . . we become human only to the extent that we take advantage of these opportunities." The observations of behaviorist B. F. Skinner indicate that we can influence social behavior in our children by shaping their social environment. Carl Jung's encouragement that we explore our most remote pasts

"Love is love's
reward."
—JOHN DRYDEN

in order to understand our potential also points to how much nurturing determines character.

I am persuaded that a loving, stimulating environment can do
a great deal to help a child develop the aspects of his or her nature
that best bring out unique talents. A positive, encouraging, nurturing setting gives a child freedom to flower and develop.

What comes to mind is my memory of Alexandra at five, decorating her own bedroom. We had moved to a larger apartment
and the girls no longer shared a room. Alexandra wanted a pale
purple floor and hot pink trim accenting white walls. We painted
the floor, walls, and trim and photographed Alexandra in her room
wearing a purple-and-pink knit dress. She got to create a world of
her own in the colors she liked best at an early age.

Alexandra is interested in becoming a journalist even though
since her early days she has shown great talent in decorating. A
child may have a talent and interest that she doesn't wish to develop
into a career. Still, these remain with her. One summer when she
was studying journalism at Northwestern University I visited her
and we went to a ten-cent store to buy supplies for her dormitory
room. She looked at the clothes hangers and said, "They won't do.
I couldn't look at that brown plastic every day."

Children of clients come to me for decorating advice and I see
that the children's point of view is largely based on the influence
of their parents. We may not see this influence for a long time and
then suddenly, as if out of the blue, we see attitudes and mannerisms
that were environmentally encouraged.

HAVE FUN

When my daughters were very young I did everything I could to
instill a sense of excitement and wonder in them about the world.
When Alexandra was in second grade I'd sometimes pick her up
at school with a balloon and a party favor bag full of little inexpensive things for her amusement. One day her math teacher noticed the pink balloon and yellow party bag and inquired, "Going

to a birthday party?" I smiled and said, "No, this is just for fun. We're spending the afternoon together." You don't have to wait for a birthday to have fun. You can create your own celebrations.

I remember that particular afternoon most vividly and what a happy time Alexandra and I had—I took pictures of her playing with her pink balloon in the sunshine near an apple tree sprinkling petals like confetti in the wind. I find I always enjoy and remember with fondness these private celebrations with my daughters. Creating your own celebrations puts the spice in life.

Good, happy memories double our life's richness. First you live an event; then you can relive it. You can create magic in your life, and with the magic you create wonderful memories.

MOTHER'S
ROLE

We are the changing generation; we can no longer look to our parents to help us solve our problems. The women of today are social pioneers. We have doors open to us that were locked tight for our mothers and grandmothers. The world is watching to see how we do. Our chance has come to make good choices, take responsibility, and gain control of our lives. We can choose not to follow old patterns, but in fact, you may find you have to make a concerted effort to change.

You now have the freedom to be fulfilled. With that freedom comes responsibility. You must take charge of your time, your health, your money, your passions. Use your power and make something extraordinary of your life. What better example for your children than a parent who makes wise choices.

I have a friend who was raised on the motto "a happy parent makes a happy child." By the time I had my daughters I had a successful career as an interior decorator and believed I had the energy and determination to do a good job raising the girls and also carry on with my career. There were moments when I was severely tested. In the late sixties lots of people thought, "Wife, mother, career—it can't work."

I'd hear questions like, "Why can't you be happy as a wife and mother? Why do you need to prove to the world that you can do it all? No one can. You have to choose." I had chosen. For me, I had to try to continue my career, raise my girls, and be a wife.

Any woman who has tried juggling marriage, children, and career knows there are times when you can keep three balls in the air. It just leaves little free time for your own leisure. A lot will depend on the flexibility of your work demands. Ideally you are your own boss but if that isn't appropriate, you should have an understanding boss. Decorating is a nurturing profession and although I enjoy commercial work I have always found my greatest fulfillment in residential work where there are children, pets, gardens, and love. I discovered I was capable of accomplishing more in a nurturing environment.

I will never forget the time my office manager took me out to lunch when I was pregnant with Alexandra. She advised me to go home permanently. "You'll never be able to live with yourself if you aren't there to watch your daughter take her first steps, Sandie. Trust me. Go home." I kept my reaction to myself, but I was upset that what she'd said would most likely be true. I spent a lot of private time thinking about this dilemma when I suddenly realized: The first step I saw my daughter take would be her first step for me. After she took one step she would take another, and then another. She would take many steps that I would get to see. It was that simple. Once I realized this I instructed the woman who was helping me care for Alexandra not to tell me if she started walking when I wasn't home but to let me make my own discoveries.

After Brooke was born I received a phone call from an in-law asking me how everything was—how was the new baby, how was Alexandra, how was my husband, and how was I? After giving a cheerful report I mentioned how hard it was for me to leave the baby to go to the office. Immediately I was asked, "Why don't you quit your job?" The question popped out as if she were inquiring whether I wanted to go to a movie.

My career, established before I married or had my daughters, was vital to me. I love my work. The truth is I could never give up my career. I've always believed I had the capacity to manage my family and my career because I have the will to make the necessary sacrifices. Family and career *are* possible if you want both badly enough and are willing to work extremely hard. There are thousands of exciting events when you have the blessing of a child to raise—if you gave up a career to watch relentlessly for each growth stage, I'm not persuaded this benefits either your child or you.

Before Brooke was born I took Alexandra on business trips. I made the practical discovery that many of my clients had children too and that the children could amuse themselves while we did some decorating. I remember arriving at a ranch in Texas with Alexandra. My client's two-year-old daughter became her playmate for three days. We showed them how to make old-fashioned valentines, they baked cookies with their baby-sitter and played in the garden, laughing, where we could keep an eye on them while we discussed colors and materials. On the weekend we all drove five hours to Santa Fe, New Mexico, munching on fried chicken.

When Brooke was born two and a half years after Alexandra, Alexandra had started nursery school and we could no longer travel together during the week. Brooke grew up hearing about the trips Alexandra had taken with me, all embellished over the years. And Alexandra has many fond memories which will influence her if she chooses to combine family and career in her adulthood.

When Brooke and Alexandra were both in nursery school I'd walk with them there to the front steps where they'd toddle up the stairs to the elevator with teachers and friends. Before school we'd usually stop off at Jimmy's Coffee Shop on Madison Avenue around the corner and get a hot chocolate or a glass of fresh squeezed orange juice. We'd blow kisses as the elevator door would close; I'd dash to the office and pick them up a few hours later.

Alexandra graduated into first grade and went up the street to the Spence School where she stayed the full day. One noon, as Brooke and I were holding hands walking home in the fresh spring

"Well begun is half done."
—*ARISTOTLE*

air, Brooke said, "Mommy, it's too bad you have to wait for me every day by the elevator. It must be so boring. I have such fun upstairs. It's not fair you have to wait around." Brooke saw me as the elevator doors closed in the morning and saw me in the same spot as the doors opened up a few hours later—what a logical thought!

I am happy that I can be an example of how to combine an interesting career with a closely knit family. Albert Schweitzer discovered "example isn't the most important thing, example is the only thing." I believe that because I maintained an exciting career throughout my daughters' entire growing-up period I have enjoyed a far richer relationship with both girls. I feel I had passion that fed both career and family. I've been able to give them pure love because I've been so happy.

We all make sacrifices for our children and for all the people we love, but giving up a career you are passionate about is not only unnecessary, it's counterproductive. I gave up many a business trip and canceled several minutes before leaving for the airport because a daughter was too sick for me to leave her. But I never lost a client because of my involvement with my daughters. On the contrary, my children have helped me in my career; they have forced me to simplify, to be practical, and have kept me in touch with reality.

THE FATHER'S ROLE

With both parents working, both parents are participating in bringing up the children. And children obviously benefit from their fathers' involvement in their development. A father who has a demanding job in the advertising world walks his children to school. A father who is an entrepreneur living in Texas works at his office the exact hours his two children are in school; that way he can take them to school, pick them up and be at home with them in the late afternoon. He goes to their sporting activities and even coaches on occasion. "I have the best possible life. I'm with my children when

"The language of truth is simple."
—SENECA

they're available, and when they're at school I work hard at the office knowing I get to be with them after school."

The more dependable help a father gives, the more outside interests and work demands a woman can assume. Talk things out. You're a team. The more openly you communicate together as loving spouses, the more smoothly you can manage.

There are only a handful of years that you have your child at home. School takes over soon enough—then there are after-school activities, tutoring, socializing. Fathers might decide that getting more actively involved with their child during the preschool years is a real priority. One father I know has a baby-sitter bring his daughter to his office for lunch twice a week. Another father takes his preschool son on shopping trips. He enjoys the company and it gives his wife some programmed free time. Take turns and have the fun with your young children. Show, through example, that your child is of utmost importance to you. Take time and add a lasting dimension to your life and to the life of your child.

EXAMPLES— ROLE MODELS

"Lives of great men [and women] all remind us We can make our lives sublime."
—HENRY WADSWORTH LONGFELLOW

Everything you do sends out signals. Your children are a mirror of you. When they are older and have learned their lessons the hard way through trial and error, they will develop their individuality. Now, they will do what you do—to an amazing degree.

If you are affectionate and open, your children will have affection for themselves and will know how to share it with others. If you are honest and trustworthy, your example will be followed. You illuminate the human struggle by your behavior and attitude— between right and wrong, good and evil. Never put yourself down, or your child or your spouse. Instead, uplift those around you. Your passionate spirit will teach your child to be imaginative in finding things to do that are interesting. Likewise, be careful not to force a child to mirror you identically. They will automatically, but your job is to encourage your child to find his or her special niche in this world.

It is rare when young children really know what they want to do when they grow up. Yet most great doctors, dancers, artists, writers, and musicians discovered their talent and love early in life and many were encouraged by a sensitive parent. If you have things that thrill you, share them with your child.

A child wants and needs a balanced life of work and love. You can't live life for your child any more than the reverse is possible. If you give up your life you will grow to become resentful and jealous of your child.

Everyone has a full life to lead. Each of us has to do something we love; we have to do something creative and fun and we have to serve others. For every choice, there is always the other side of the coin. You make difficult choices, and if you decide to stay home don't complain.

Other people will give you advice based on their own circumstances—this has no relevance to your life. Choose to keep whatever power you've worked to acquire. You will have the strength to make the right decisions when you are completely honest with yourself. If you aren't working full-time, take a course at school. Do volunteer work. We've all heard stories of the woman who became a lawyer at fifty or who started a career as a filmmaker after her children were grown. What is your dream? Identify it and pursue it; this will encourage your children to follow theirs. You may find new vitality just by volunteering at a nearby hospital, or working part-time at a boutique. Try your hand at painting, sculpting, writing, decorating, consulting, weaving—be the person you were before you had children. Remember, you are a pioneer. You have to chart a new course.

TRUST YOUR OWN INSTINCTS

Learn to trust your gut feeling. Shakti Gawain, author of *Living in the Light*, writes, "Our children essentially need two things from us: 1) They need to be recognized for who they really are. 2) They need us to create an example for them of how to live effectively in the world of form. . . . In return for taking responsibility for these two things, we receive from our children endless amounts of vibrant, alive energy . . . because they have not yet developed much rational censorship, they are almost totally intuitive, completely spontaneous, and absolutely honest."

When you open up to the truth inside you, you'll intuitively sense your child's needs. You'll be there when you're needed. You can't be told by someone else; you will already know.

PAY ATTENTION

Children are starved for their parents' attention. We all get distracted and busy, but when a child needs our attention, we should give it. Observe your child. If you have more than one child you will immediately discover how different they are. Avoid labeling them—Johnny is the athlete of the family and Barbara is the brain. Never let a child hear these remarks. Each child develops at an individual pace and changes with each growth period. Remain open to discover the many secrets your child will reveal to you. When you see a new interest emerge, encourage your child to pursue new discoveries.

Keep track of their activities. Have a tab in your Filofax or organization book for each child and make personal notes of schedules, classes, and vacations. This way you can be attuned to specific activities and dates that are coming up.

Each child is unique and your attention should be individual. Don't assume they should both do the same activities. You may cause unnecessary sibling rivalry.

Pay attention! Gems will be revealed.

LISTEN TO THEIR OPINIONS

Your children want you to listen. Try to put yourself in their place and when you hear them, take action. When I was eight years old I told my mother the pay telephone booth in my elementary school was too high for the students to reach. Mother was an interior designer and took my observation to heart and the telephone was lowered.

Ask questions. Bring out more insights. Children have clear vision and feel things spontaneously. Encourage your child to express opinions and share observations. Parents who do are richer for it. Look at your child when he expresses himself. When he is finished speaking, let him know you are pleased. The more anxiety-free, calm time you give your child to express thoughts, the more articulate he will become and the more at ease he will feel communicating with others.

I've found that listening to my daughters has added a great deal to my life. Once when we were redecorating our living room I was trying to decide on a color for our walls to go with a yellow-background chintz. I was flirting with pale green and we all got in on the act. Alexandra yelled, "No! Pale, pale pink." Our walls are now lacquered this incredibly pale peony color and they have given us and our friends a great deal of pleasure.

Another time she suggested large panels of mirrors on the walls on either side of our fireplace. By installing mirrors we opened up the space and gained light, and the two windows in our living room reflect in the mirrors, creating the illusion of four windows.

Brooke often comes into the room where I prepare my lectures. When all the slides are set up on the light box she studies them, eliminating the images that are repetitious or not strong enough. I am often struck by the depth of perception and understanding my daughters reveal when they help me.

Every experience teaches us firsthand.

A house is supported by four walls. As an interior designer I always think of walls and individual rooms when I think of the structure. Studies indicate that a well-structured home life is the best environment for the development of human potential.

Children today yearn for structure. The stronger the parents'

STRUCTURE

confidence in the positive values necessary to nurture individuality, the clearer the message will be to their children. So, the house has structure and there are house rules. Your children can help out around the house, learning to share responsibility. The healthy habits a child develops at home will be with him throughout his life.

Here are a few household rules we developed to give structure to our home.

- *Mood Attitude.* No one is allowed to be grumpy and pollute the atmosphere of our home. If someone is out of sorts, he or she retires to a bedroom to recover or goes for a walk; everyone is expected to make an effort. Bad moods are contagious and it is selfish to behave in a negative way that tears down others.

- *No Whining.* We have a rule that whining is not permitted in the house. We told the girls when they were very young that there are no "eh" signs in the English language. We would not tolerate negative attention-getting techniques and made it clear we meant business.

- *Family Meals.* Children need to sit down to a table and eat a proper breakfast with their parents. This is an opportunity to share affection and while enjoying eating breakfast together, positive values are being reinforced. You can offer encouragement to a child who is trying out for a team or taking a test. Don't skip being a family at breakfast.

  Eating habits and table manners are vitally important. Except when you go out in the evenings, eat with your children. They learn from you and when you combine interesting conversation with good food and good table manners, a child learns the pleasures of civility.

- *Time Schedule.* Foster individuality by offering scheduled free time at home for your child to develop personal interests. Have weekly chores that must be done and then leave your child alone to have time to discover.

Character. Stress character.

Establish a time your child goes to bed. Children lack experience and when they get tired they get discouraged. They need lots of sleep in order to keep the discipline of their academic schedules.

- *Telephone.* Limit the times your child is allowed to talk on the telephone. Set up telephone times and post a schedule in the kitchen. When a child is studying, the telephone should be off limits.

- *Reading.* Reading for pleasure, not just when assigned, is enriching. Encourage your child to sit with you and read. Besides being fun to read together as a family, it encourages a lifelong reading habit very early.

- *Television.* Set up strict limits on television. We were blessed because our children's school had a ruling that students were not allowed to watch television on weekdays. Parents should set up their own restrictions on television viewing. If you watch television a great deal yourself, your child will follow suit. You can tell far better stories than the producers of network television. So tell stories to your children and entertain yourself in the process.

- *Spirituality.* Make every effort to expose your child to weekly religious training. Discuss faith in your home and nurture your child's beliefs in a presence in their life greater than their own.

- *Fitness.* Exercise is essential to a child in developing a healthy mind, body, and spirit. Early training in a sport will be a powerful lesson all through life. A child can experience joy from the discipline and self-development a sport demands.

These are just some of the ways you can create structure for your children. When you show your love and caring through patterns of discipline at home, your children will not be restricted; rather, they will thrive.

"Diligence is the mother of good fortune."
—*MIGUEL DE CERVANTES*

155

RESPECTING
INDIVIDUAL
INTERESTS
AND GIFTS

One of the most exciting aspects of bringing a child into the world is to discover and explore inherited talents in your child. If he becomes interested in music, dance, science, medicine, tennis, pottery, art, or writing you can encourage the spark of interest by providing the necessary elements. Whatever it takes—lessons, trips to the natural history museum, a place to practice—show your concern and take action. It's also worth encouraging your child to do things he or she isn't good at, just for the joy of it. For example, I am no ballerina. My sister Barbara loved ballet, and I also was given a pair of pink satin toe shoes and provided with lessons at my request. After several months of practice, parents were allowed to come see their daughters perform. My great-aunt made me a pink tutu. I must have been seven. I remember thrusting myself across the floor, imagining I was a bird—my hair was in a bun, I wore pink rouge and lipstick. I felt so graceful and loved the whole experience of performing—fluttering, bowing. Mother encouraged this kind of fantasy and each of us discovered our strengths and talents and were allowed at the same time to enjoy ourselves in a variety of other activities.

But overprogramming a child is a mistake. Each child has a certain capacity for these extra activities. Be guided by your child. The best bet is to expose and observe, then see what clicks. Not every child has to grow up playing the piano or playing tennis. Keep an open mind to interests and hobbies you haven't pursued. Children go through rapid changes. I remember just before Alexandra learned to read she spent all her free time painting colorful abstracts that were highly artistic and well executed. She developed an Expressionist style and created swirling forms in black outline, meticulously filling in the shapes with vibrant primary colors. She enjoyed her artwork and we provided pads of heavy-duty paper and broad-tip color markers.

We have the power to teach our children the true meaning of success and not to fear failure.

A well-known American writer confessed to me he hasn't submitted a manuscript to his literary agent in four years. "I haven't written anything good enough," he explained. When I reminded him he has received two literary prizes and has published five books and a hundred articles, he smiled. "I'm afraid of failure."

I have a friend who lovingly told me of her mother's advice when she was debating whether or not to try out for cheerleading. Her mother sat Deborah down and asked what she wanted to do. "I want to try out, but I'm afraid I won't make it." Her mother told her that she would fail only if she didn't try. When you do your best you can't lose. Deborah practiced the week before tryouts and didn't make the cheerleading team. Several of her friends tried out with her and also didn't make it. They decided to try out for soccer and didn't make that team, either. Discouraged, Deborah went back to her mother for advice. "What should I do? I'm a failure," she fretted as her mother listened attentively. Then, tenderly, her mother reminded her that she was a stronger person than she had been before the tryouts. "Trying is what's important."

Trying, being curious and courageous, is how we learn just what we can do. Children need us to show them how much effort goes into our successes, how many false starts and setbacks it takes. You are doing a child a disservice to let him think life is easy—if it were easy it wouldn't be so exciting.

Children need to be encouraged to count their gains, not their losses. They succeed when they reach out in kindness to another person, when they genuinely care about the well-being of a friend, when they make an effort to try new things. It's no accident that a favorite childhood story is "The Little Engine That Could." When you think you can, you have a goal and work toward that goal. Striving is all. Tell your children about the joy of being engaged in something that requires this best effort, about being able to push themselves hard and then feeling the satisfaction of trying. Advise them to edit the activities they don't find worthwhile so they can concentrate on things that give them inner satisfaction. Together, you and your children can develop their confidence and strength. There is no greater gift you can give them.

COMPETITION

Make a little masterpiece of life each day.

Some people are so fiercely competitive they lose out on the joy of social sports and social life. Tennis was my great passion growing up but my father was disappointed that I lacked "the killer instinct." What I discovered, to my own delight, was that I enjoy challenging myself more than beating others.

The late interior designer Angelo Donghia came to a decorator's showhouse where I had done a room. He looked around and congratulated me and said, "Sandie, you're doing a great job. There are too few of us and too many who need us. I'm so proud of you." I was a young, relatively undiscovered designer at the time and his support and kindness did a great deal to encourage me.

We must reinforce our children's efforts to try hard and to stretch beyond what is comfortable, without comparing them to others. Schools use tests to evaluate where a student will fit into their curriculum. What they can't determine from the tests is compassion, kindness, caring for others, love of beauty, spirituality, enthusiasm.

We live in a competitive world. There's no getting around that fact. But let's say the Smiths beat you in mixed doubles. Did you still have fun? How about simply enjoying the process of playing tennis?

Your children are watching you. Be a good sport. No one wins all the time. Sometimes we lose out on something we think is terribly important only to discover we were spared because it wasn't right for us.

Another form of competition often arises between siblings. Sibling rivalry can be diverted. Our daughters have an exceptionally close bond and, other than fighting over the mustard stain on a white silk blouse or the black jacket borrowed without permission, they get along well. When they were very young they flew together unaccompanied by an adult to Los Angeles to visit their father. When I left them on the plane I had a lump in my throat that wouldn't go away and they discovered a simple truth: they had each other.

When the girls were two and four we moved into a larger apartment and they had their own rooms for the first time. What should have been a treat was perceived as a punishment, not a privilege. They'd end up sleeping in the same bed! Now they share friends, clothes, and confidences. There is no jealousy between them. Brooke and Alexandra have diverse views and opinions, different interests and talents, and their love of each other is really an expansion of who each one is individually. How rare and wonderful this relationship is between sisters. But it *can* happen.

When Frank Boyden was the headmaster at Deerfield Academy he told a group of seniors who had just been accepted at Yale, "Finish up strong, boys." Henry Wadsworth Longfellow once wrote, "Great is the art of beginning, but greater is the art of ending."

Discipline is a dynamic that helps us to keep going whether we're in the mood or not. Dancers are disciplined, so are singers and actors. In fact, most people you and I respect are highly disciplined. We see the results of their accomplishments, and if they've really knocked themselves out trying, their work looks effortless. What we're not seeing is all their pain and perseverance.

When I was growing up my mother said discipline should become a habit because it frees you to plan your time. You know what you're going to do, and everything else you eliminate. Decisions become easy as you pursue what interests you.

In *The Road Less Traveled*, M. Scott Peck talks about delaying gratification and describes this tool of discipline as "a process of

SEEING SOMETHING THROUGH

"A journey of a thousand miles must begin with a single step."
—LAO-TSU

scheduling the pain and pleasure of life in such a way as to enhance the pleasure by meeting and experiencing the pain first and getting it over with." Once involved in a project your child will discover the delight in it, but dreading something because it isn't fun or putting it off until he's cornered gives a child low self-esteem. Help your child so that minor daily chores don't appear overwhelming. Each task seen through adds a layer to your child's inner potential.

If you see that a child has bitten off too much and is getting bogged down, help with the scheduling. Possibly he needs a break to refresh his spirit before tackling the rest of his math.

Children at an early age realize that they, not their parents, are responsible for their schoolwork and the larger picture, their own lives. Children want their parents to teach necessary discipline so they can know how to be responsible for living their own lives. However, a parent who bails out a child from undone homework is making a mistake. Far better to see to it that television is off limits, way in advance of the assignment due. Responsibility gives power to individuality.

COMMUNI-
CATION

Philosophy professor Allan Bloom in his book *The Closing of the American Mind* made quite clear the dismal state of our education today. Bloom notes that in the past the family was the true seat of religious training and that the impulse to educate flowed from it. He believes one of the reasons today's students come to the university with no sense of "the great revelations, epics, and philosophies" is "the dreariness of the family's landscape. . . . People sup together, play together, travel together, but they don't think together."

If we become open enough to communicate honestly with our children we will give them a great gift they will take with them wherever they journey in their lives. Yet, many parents are too busy to read and find writing too difficult. Television becomes the tranquilizer, soothing our nerves from the demands outside the home. I made a study recently of a class of high school graduates and discovered that only one out of fifty students had written a thank-you letter for a graduation gift. You may think that is merely poor manners but I disagree. Many people become nearly paralyzed at the thought of expressing their feelings in words. We parents must create a physical environment that is conducive to sharing thoughts, ideas, feelings, and love.

Emphasize reading, writing, and speaking in your home. Don't let a child giggle and say, "I'm too shy." Shyness can be overcome. Encourage your child to try out for the debating team. If you have a funny child, encourage her to try out for an improvisational group or to start one of her own. Get your children to give toasts at family gatherings and to recite poetry or prose at the dinner table. Have them take turns saying grace or a blessing or a thank-you to God for a sunny day. Peter asked his eleven-year-old son Nathaniel to say grace before Thanksgiving dinner and after a brief silence he looked down at his plate piled with food: "Thank you, God, for the turkey with stuffing and gravy, for the scalloped potatoes, the squash, peas, and carrots. Oh, and for my family. Amen."

Obviously nonverbal communication is terribly important and observation is the beginning of communication. Make a real effort to talk at meals when you're together. Discourage earphones when children and parents are together. Talk during car trips. If a child is daydreaming, inquire what wonderful thoughts he is thinking. Encourage your child to express himself.

When a young child says something amazing—"God is crying now, Mommy. That's why it's raining"—write it down in a little pocket book and give these thoughts back to your child on his or her sixteenth birthday.

Encourage your child to announce things in assembly, to act, to perform. Mothers who don't do public speaking must work hard to help a daughter overcome a fear of public speaking. Women today, no matter what they do, need to be able to speak in front of others.

Our children will hold great power if they can communicate

well with others. Stress reading, writing, and talking as the tools that will free them to make a real contribution in the future.

"I NEED
LOVE"
When Brooke graduated from Spence School she put an advertisement in the yearbook saying good-bye to friends and parents. Her message to me was, "I will miss you, Mom, telling me 'I need love.'" We love out of a need to share. I realize my own need for love and so I reach out to hug someone else!

When love is demonstrated in even the smallest way, it can bring joy. "I need love" always works in our family. After Brooke hugs me she tells Peter, "Mom needs more love." This is my way of encouraging other people to show affection toward me. A good bear hug has mysterious power. It's love in action.

Touch is fundamental to the communication of love. Helen Keller, blind and deaf from a young age, wrote in her diary, "Paradise is attained by touch" after she and her dog Lo had played together.

We know that children who have the most physical contact with their parents or care givers walk and talk earlier and have higher I.Q.s. Nothing is more important to early physical and mental growth than touching.

Of course, when children get older they often go through stages of rejecting a parent's touch, usually during puberty when the child becomes sexually aware. "Stop being queer" is a sign to back off a bit. Boys feel awkward with an overbearing mother but there are lots of ways to show love and affection without grabbing a son and squeezing him. A smile, a pat on the back, thumbs up, a handshake—whatever works for both of you.

In addition to lots of hugs and kisses, soft dolls and stuffed animals can be loving substitutes. When I was a little girl I had a huge soft teddy bear, and photographs show me endlessly hugging "Teddy." Peter loves these early pictures and one day came home with a little teddy bear he thought was identical to the one I spent so much of my childhood hugging. I am happy to have a teddy bear again! He sits on a loveseat at the foot of the bed among lots of flowery and embroidered pillows and is held by the girls when they sit down to chat with us when we're in our bed. Having a soft teddy bear around can be a sweet psychological comfort.

The comfort and security of a stuffed animal come from memories of childhood, but the feelings are still there when you grow up. Laura was a senior at St. Paul's School when she took her senior study project at my design firm. We did a bit of traveling during those two months and flew to Albuquerque, New Mexico, to work in an adobe house for an architect and her husband. Because the house was under construction my client arranged for us to stay at one of the condominiums her architectural firm built. We got there late at night and were freezing cold. Laura had said good night and was in her bedroom. There was a fireplace in my bedroom so I built a fire. The smell of the firewood brought her out to investigate and confess, "There aren't any sheets on my bed." I quickly turned down my bed to check if it had sheets. "This one does, and it's king size, so we can both fit. You're welcome to sleep in here with the warmth of the fire." We had to get up in five hours to drive to the airport in our rented car to catch our plane and we didn't have the energy to make up her bed. Laura left to get something and returned with a stuffed doll she'd slept with since she was four. "I can't sleep without my friend."

"But headlong joy is ever on the wing."
—JOHN MILTON

Children will respect us if we are not afraid to set standards. Being a parent is not a popularity contest. Respect, like trust, has to be earned. If you have honestly respected your children, you will see that respect coming back to you.

Honor your child. Show consideration and appreciation. We were always reprimanded as children by strict parents who were trying to teach us everything we needed to know to face the real world. Our parents failed to respect our greatness and our spirits

MUTUAL RESPECT

to the full potential. They punished, used force, and told us how we failed. They left many of us with low self-esteem.

I don't regret my parents' strict rules. But I do wish more parents would praise a child's beautiful thoughts or sensitive ways, because we grow when we are recognized for doing some things right. If we honor and respect each other, we can grow stronger together in an atmosphere of love and support.

We honor our children when we show concern.

THEIR FRIENDS

Our children will make their own friends. Make their friends welcome in your household. Not every friend will become one for life but some will. Children are thrown together with other boys and girls their age and they socialize. Respect their selection of friends.

Be yourself but be your best self. You are representing your child and your child wants to feel proud of you. Take your cues from your child: when you hear, "Katie just adores you and has so much fun with you, Mom. She really wants to see more of you," you know you can relax and be affectionate with Katie. If you have a teenage son whose roommate at boarding school stays up drinking brandy with you until 3 A.M. discussing Lawrence Durrell, I think your son has reason to wish you'd gone to bed at 11 P.M. with your spouse!

Children rarely have the security and self-esteem they will grow into as adults. Be sensitive to their potential embarrassment about almost everything. Children outgrow this eventually but until they do be aware of the delicacy of their emotions. Remember, you have your own friends. Let your children have theirs.

SOCIAL LIFE

Let's not forget we were young once and liked going out on the town. Our children feel omnipotent; the world is theirs, nothing can ever happen to them. We know better. We want our children to be safe at the same time we want them to have friends and a social life independent from their family.

"Do you know where your children are?" You should know your children's whereabouts and they should know yours. In our household we believe in the honor system, and I never assume my children are lying to me. We have a rule that the girls leave the name, phone number, and address of where they are when they spend the night at a friend's house.

Have your home be a loving gathering place for children to socialize. We turned our dark-red English library into a blue-and-white wicker room that has the atmosphere of a summer beach house so the girls can entertain their friends informally, watch movies, and listen to music.

When the children are at our house I feel relaxed, knowing they are safe. Offer to have parties and encourage their friends to join you at mealtimes. Let your children's friends spend the night—even if it means using sleeping bags. Children don't need ironed, scented sheets and a four-poster bed. Be flexible and open up your house to your children and their friends as a priority. We feel our most wonderful parties have been given for their friends, and we love seeing sleepy bodies emerge from different rooms when they smell the morning coffee.

Be great in your love.

CURFEWS

Children shouldn't be let loose to con their parents into doing exactly what they want. With both parents working it is crucial that they know where their children are and vice versa. Our daughters come in to our bedroom and let us know they're home safe every night they go out. If they are going to be late, even five minutes after their curfew, they call and explain or negotiate. If they can't reach us, they get right home.

Be strict. Mean business. Synchronize your watches: 12:30 A.M. is 12:30 sharp. Late curfews should be for very special events, not the rule.

If children are going to a rock concert, insist on having someone pick them up. Riots happen. Make your daughter promise she will never travel alone. Be sure she has enough cash tucked away for an emergency each time she goes out. Have an account with a radio taxi so, if needed, she can be picked up and taken home door to door. Don't assume her dates know how dangerous it is for an attractive young lady out on the street. Stay up and greet your child. If you doze off, wake up and talk, ask how the evening was. Some of the best talks I've ever had with the girls have taken place when they've returned home from a date.

DRUGS AND ALCOHOL

I have never taken a drug. I have seen enough to persuade me that drugs are a form of suicide, a living death. Statistics indicate that most of America's children try drugs. Many of you will face the horror and agony of a child who is bored and unhappy and wants a quick fix. I pray you are spared.

Talk about drugs with your children. Buy books about drugs. Go to school discussions. Watch special programs on television with your children. Make it clear that your house is drug-free and under no circumstances will any kind of drug be tolerated. Be sure your child has that clear: if a son or daughter decides to take drugs, he or she is no longer welcome to live at home. Home is where there is a family, and certain standards. The child on drugs can utterly destroy the harmony of a home. Be serious and be ready to act. Drugs destroy not only the vitality and spirit of the person using them, but also of those close by.

Alcohol doesn't have to destroy lives. Expose your children to wine and beer in your home. In moderation, alcohol can be a pleasant addition to social occasions. However, it is crucial that children learn how to limit and control their drinking, or quit. If a child of yours comes home and has had too much to drink, make it a point to discuss it calmly the next day, not when you will receive irrational excuses and denial.

We teach our children through our example.

When children are young they love to imitate their parents. Let young children fold clothes, the older ones iron. Even if you have help in the house there are plenty of projects for children to do with you. Let your children help you set the table for a party or holiday. Have them help decorate the house for Christmas. Clean out the attic together, go together to town to pick up a rake, do the marketing, plant the roses, make grape jelly.

Your children don't need toys that are imitations of adult equipment; get the real thing but scaled down—buy a real broom and a real mop. Cut down the handle if need be. Cut a dust rag in two. Prepare your child for life with real tools. At the appropriate time buy a used typewriter for your child.

By involving children in your life, they will also learn about priorities. I remember one occasion when Brooke took charge of my time. The nursery school she attended would safety-pin notes to the children's sweaters to notify us about special events. On one occasion Brooke decided she would take charge and remove her note. A festive Christmas party was coming up where the children performed for their parents and homemade refreshments were served. On the big day of the party I was oblivious. Everyone asked Brooke, "Where's your Mommy?" "My Mom's too busy. She's giving my sister and me a party tonight," she answered calmly. When I picked her up from school and discovered there had been a party I hadn't heard about I was slightly embarrassed but very touched. Brooke at age four was protecting my time!

One way of involving your children in your life is by taking them with you on business ventures where you feel it's appropriate. While I'm certain Mrs. Brown knew I spent as much time with Alexandra as I could, I never came out and told her that I took my little girl with me on most of my business trips those first few years before she went to school. I do remember once being called into the office of the business manager. She frowned. "Now, Sandie, you have been seen during working hours with a baby. This be-

Make moments worth remembering.

167

havior has to stop." I'd been caught by one of the senior decorators in a fancy chandelier shop on Fifty-seventh Street with Alexandra in my arms. This may have been a real scandal in those days; however, in my life it was a necessity, and I mention it to show how you can involve a child in your career. You'll be surprised what a child can learn just by being around you while you do the things you love.

One winter weekend Alexandra visited my mother in Connecticut. My mother took Alexandra to her design studio Saturday morning and amused her by letting her loose with fabric and paint swatches—something Alexandra has played with since the cradle. Mother was lost in her projects and glanced down on the floor from her desk. "Are you okay, dear?" Alexandra said, "Not really, Ninny. There isn't a good pink in this whole swatch book." Mother was amazed, got up out of her chair, sat on the floor to examine the fabric book, and admitted her granddaughter was right. Alexandra at age five knew her pinks.

MONEY   I believe Tolstoy was right that the two important things in life are love and work. Don't worry about leaving money to your children. Spend money on them now, when they are dependent on you for support. When they are adults, let them earn their own money through their chosen work. To me, money is most delicious when it is the result of hard work. I feel that money can be potentially dangerous if given too freely when a child is too young. Ideally, at a certain age, each of us should earn our own money.

Education opens doors and introduces fields of interest and pleasure. If parents provide money for a good education and reasonable operating expenses, a child is free to pick up the ball and run with it. I have had a thrilling time earning my own way. There is a creative tension that is exhilarating when you take risks and you have no one to blame but yourself. When you do succeed you have earned your success through effort and willpower.

Motivation is something that is hard to instill in a child. Furnish your child with the right educational diet and through your own example let him observe the fun you're having with your own rewards from hard work. The process will be contagious.

Remember, money is not love. Love is.

Children need to get away from the world just as much as adults do, maybe more. Honor your children's privacy. Never barge into their bedroom.

PRIVACY

Trust is earned.

Children need a place of their own where they can think and daydream, try on clothes, do makeup, practice shaving, fantasize, be goofy. They should not be disturbed. Alone, a child can stretch the powers of imagination and sort things out. A child learns how to enjoy being alone if you as a parent make it a positive, pleasant experience.

A DO NOT DISTURB sign means total isolation. A closed door means please knock. Don't criticize a child for sleeping during the day. Lying in bed, listening to gentle music is a way of calming down after a hard, demanding day at school.

Once your child is a toddler let him be in charge of arranging and decorating. Having someone come in and revamp things behind your back is a violation and very upsetting. Once a doll or a stuffed animal has been loved, like the Velveteen Rabbit it becomes real and is part of us. Respect the things your children have become attached to. When Brooke redecorated her bedroom we turned her closet into a dressing room. It now looks like a clothing boutique. In clearing out the accumulation of stuff to create the new design we discovered a menagerie of her stuffed animals and dolls, including her favorite, Snoopy. Knowing the dolls bring back fond memories for the girls, I have scattered them about in our linen closet. When we reach for a towel or a roll of toilet paper they give all of us a little smile.

BOUNDARIES What do you tell your children? I have never discussed my sexual life with my children, nor would I answer a direct personal question if I were asked. It is none of their business nor anyone else's outside of my bedroom. Children must learn about mystery and fantasy, and telling all is never a good idea. Most children until eighteen or twenty can't be trusted with a confidence. They'll go tell their friends at school and exaggerate.

HAPPY VS. We should strive to be happy, not perfect. Children need to learn
PERFECT to try hard to succeed but not be unreasonably hard on themselves. People who achieve success and are enthusiastic about life learn to accept what is, and make the most of what they have been given. Making the most of our time, our resources, and our talents requires a healthy degree of acceptance.

Show your children your vulnerability as well as your strength. You aren't perfect and you won't raise perfect children. You and your children can live happy, healthy, normal lives.

DIVORCE When two adults decide to get divorced, they both tend to act like children. Nah, nah, nah, nah, nah—the bickering goes back and forth. While many parents remain married "for the sake of the children," once they talk divorce, they become childish and ugly.

Never involve your child in any kind of a marriage dispute. Fight your own fights in private. Encourage your child to maintain a close relationship with your former spouse. Bitterness is unattractive and dangerous to your health. There were lots of good times. No one is all bad. Nothing is more real or wonderful than the simple pleasures of a family whose strength comes from building each other up. Try to remember that your child is innocent and needs love and the assurance that one parent is not abandoning him.

When I reached thirty-three, Alexandra had a fear I was going to die because Jesus died at thirty-three. I was touched that my seven-year-old daughter put me in the same league as Jesus, but I understood that for her the association was very powerful.

When my mother died and we arrived back at the apartment after her funeral, Brooke sat on my lap and said, "I'm fat." She was expressing sadness over the death of her grandmother by feeling fat.

Most of us have trouble with the concept of death. Each of us has to come to the acceptance that we will die. Death is a reminder that life is a precious gift. It sharpens our focus and helps us to live more vibrantly. The man who married Peter and me, John Bowen Coburn, former Bishop of Massachusetts, wrote a book about the loss of his infant daughter who died suddenly in her crib. In his book, *Anne and the Sand Dobbies*, he told his surviving children: "One thing I do know is that you can't be a lone wolf in heaven. You can't even be a lone wolf here. You belong to other people, and they belong to you. The whole point of living is that you're with people and that you love people and some love you. . . . [Anne] now lives in a better, new world. It's a spiritual world. That's why heaven is like loving. If all you are is spirit and that spirit is love, you can't help loving all the time."

When C. S. Lewis's wife died of cancer he was assailed by indecision and self-pity. "I know that the thing I want is exactly the thing I can never get." Lewis came to recognize that "bereavement is a universal and integral part of our experience of love."

Children should be told that the dead person's body is dead. The body will never come alive and we will miss the person who is gone. We can continue to love someone who has died and because of that love, there can be positive spiritual communion with the other person. I travel with my mother, we talk during the day, we share a great deal together, and she died eight years ago.

Remind your child that many people before us have died. And sweetest of all, after someone physically dies, they live on in our minds.

Encourage your child to write a sympathy letter to a friend who has lost someone in death. It helps him to sympathize and remember the shared good times. Remind your child that the person who has died is in no physical pain. We who are left behind feel the sadness of our loss.

DON'T WORRY

Parents tend to worry about every little detail of child rearing— toilet training, naps, teething, schedules; we agonize over leafy greens and nutrition. Education anxiety starts when we worry over which pre-play group our child will get into. We become so concerned about whether we're doing the right thing that we can overlook the obvious: the most nourishing secret of all is honest, true, unqualified love. Worry, to my knowledge, never helps and it makes a child nervous to experience an anxious parent.

STRENGTH

It is during the most difficult times that your strength must appear. My friend Kate was at her office one morning and received a telephone call that her apartment was on fire. She panicked as she looked at her watch wondering if her infant son was safe with his nanny for their morning outing in Central Park or caught in the fire. Imagine her anxiety as she arrived at the apartment building to be greeted by fire engines, police, and dozens of neighbors and curious watchers. She was blessed—her nurse arrived with Kate's son in his carriage seconds later, oblivious to the fire. After two days of shock and despair, Kate and her husband vowed to put their lives back together. Their son is too young to appreciate his parents' strength, but he will discover it as the years go on.

Look for quality in people and things.

I have always told the girls that I don't know what I would do if anything ever happened to either one of them. I live each day knowing how painful it must be for parents to lose a child—a pain I have never experienced personally.

Our children need us to be strong. Make it your slogan: "Parents Are Strong. Period." We need to set an example of how, though we experience severe pain and suffer great agony, at the same time we accept our loss. We have to rise above the pain we experience and try to be useful.

I remember once when Brooke was about ten and was running a high fever. She was hallucinating, and she kept poking her fingers at my eyes. I began to fall apart. Peter told me all children who have high fevers act this way and not to worry. When her fever went down she became herself again. I pulled myself together and saw her through the illness. The focus must be on the child.

Children want to be able to come to us for strength. We're missing out on opportunities to be helpful if we don't have a reserve of strength to deal with unexpected problems.

LOOSEN UP

Kid around with your child. Show him how much fun life can be. Laugh. Be silly and funny as well as serious and strict. Show all the dimensions of life. Run out in the rain together. Take a drive. Do somersaults down a grassy hill. Have a picnic. Play catch. Go on a bike ride. Take a night off and escape to a country inn together. Go to a library and browse. Go to the ice-cream parlor and split a chocolate milk shake. Take time to enjoy your child each day.

Listen to the wisdom of your child.

The energy required to celebrate life together gets replenished the more fun we generate. Don't miss an opportunity to have a good time. Do things on your children's level. Let them know you're a real person, not just an authority figure. Let their joys rub off on your spirit and vice versa. You can gain wisdom by understanding the beauty of youth and the free spirits of your children.

Turn potential dullness into fun. When the girls were younger we would attack the messes in their room by getting huge garbage bags and "de-thugging." I decided the choice was to dread cleaning up or do it with a silly, ironic twist. I'd inquire, "What has happened here? A tornado or a hurricane?" We'd giggle as we turned chaos into order.

Whether it's taking a bath, having lunch, cooking, driving your child to school, each routine can be an occasion for fun. Loosen up a bit and rejoice in your love of your children. Grab one and give her a hug. Send an "I care" package through the mail. Make a bouquet of field flowers and place it next to your child's bed. Write a love letter and place it on his or her pillow. Sit on your daughter's bed and rap awhile. Be a friend—you are your son or daughter's mother, that doesn't go away, but be a friend also. Share your memories of being his age and the silly things that happened to you.

ESTABLISHING FAMILY TRADITIONS

The traditions we have as a family bring us a great deal of pleasure and we know that whatever happens, we can always look forward to them. I particularly like Christmastime with its feelings of generosity, felicity, and grace. It is a giving and sharing time that brings us back to real values.

Once we had children, we created traditions that symbolize the Christmas season. We always have a tree-trimming gathering a week before Christmas. We still hang on the tree the rather tattered ornaments the girls made in the fourth and fifth grades. They recall the school friends with whom they made them as they reminisce about past Christmases. Our tree has never been sophisticated, or one that a magazine would want to photograph. But it rings true for us, and we love its specialness. Each year we have a family Christmas party, a tradition that started when the children were in play school. People come and put a little present under the tree, usually something they've made or grown. This year a friend brought us some narcissus tied in red ribbon which she'd nurtured from bulbs on her kitchen window ledge.

We have a large family and Christmas is a hectic time of year, so we deliberately plan a family dinner several weeks before Christmas when we get together to celebrate one another. We have favorite dishes we all select—a leg of lamb and vegetable casserole. We give presents, take pictures, and spend unhurried hours enjoying one another.

On Thanksgiving and Easter we go to church before having a lovely dinner at home. Friends and family share in the work. Someone brings dessert, someone else brings an assortment of cheese.

Every August we have a family summer cocktail party. Everyone gathers, looking tan and healthy, and we have an opportunity to catch up before people go away in the fall. The girls invite their friends who in turn are asked to bring their parents. We have our friends and they bring their children. A friend who is a professional photographer marks her calendar so she can be with us to take lots of pictures which we send to the families with a note.

Traveling together as a family has brought us lasting happy memories. When the girls were younger, every summer we would plan a special trip together. Before we'd go, we'd read about the place we planned to visit, and discuss our trip at mealtimes. When Alexandra and Brooke were six and eight and Peter's son Nathaniel was fourteen, we went to Greece and each of us kept a diary. Brooke needed help, so I took dictation. Before we left we had looked at travel posters and brochures plus pretty picture books and we asked Brooke what she thought Greece looked like.

"The sky is blue, blue, blue, and the water is blue, blue, blue, blue!" she said.

And of course she was right! When Brooke graduated from high school she went back to Greece with friends as a graduation present. She loved looking through our Greek Family Odyssey to help her memory of where she'd been so many years ago.

By recording the trip and taking lots of pictures we share memories and are able to relive the pleasure over and over in our minds.

Because we established a tradition of taking a trip together every summer, the question at the dinner table would be "Where?" One year when the girls were teenagers they took charge of planning a trip to California. Peter and I had the best time having them in charge. They did all the research on where to stay and where to eat, and they made all the reservations. Because of the wonderful trips we've taken together, we all love to travel and we feel comfortable and exhilarated in new and unfamiliar places.

Trips with your children don't have to be expensive. Go camping, go skiing, go to a deserted beach. Take the lead from your children and listen to what might be meaningful to them. My parents drove from Connecticut to Florida over Christmas vacations with four children so I could play in the Orange Bowl tennis tournament and take tennis lessons from Doris Hart. My family teases me to this day that it was a long drive, but we have wonderful memories.

Vacations—when the telephone doesn't ring and there is no television—can be the times you remember the most, looking back. You and your children can relax together, seeing historical sights, experiencing the wonders of nature, whatever's on the agenda. These shared experiences will become your children's real capital from their memories as they grow up.

RECREATION

Encourage your children to find an individual sport they can pursue on their own. Swimming, bowling, croquet, ice skating, classical dance, horseback riding, or tap dancing—it doesn't really matter what the activity is as long as your child takes action and tries something that sounds like fun.

Have lots of outings and things you do as a family. You can all go to museums on a rainy day, or to the theater, ballet, a concert, an opera, the movies. Watch old movies at home, barbecue a chicken supper, drive to the beach, take a van and go to see the foliage in New England in late October. Pick blueberries in Massachusetts in

"Dost thou love life? Then do not squander time; for that's the stuff life is made of."
—*BENJAMIN FRANKLIN*

July. Go to Williamsburg, Virginia. Make old-fashioned valentines and send them to the old and young you adore. Bake cookies and cakes and send them in tins to everyone you miss who is living a distance away. Go to Washington to brush up on your country's heritage.

Write a list of all the activities you'd like to do in the next six months. Ask your children to make their list. Then if you find you're having a blah day, whip out your list—there will be suggestions of things to do that will delight you. There's the book you've been dying to read. Or that nature walk you've been meaning to take. Get out and about and *do* something. You will emerge a renewed and different person and so will your child.

Reward a child's special talents and interests. Brooke when she was seven became a Sunday painter. She spread out her drop cloth on the hall floor, put on a smock, and painted flowers. If she didn't like the vase the tulips were in she'd rearrange the flowers and paint away. She imitated the style of Roger Mŭhl's thick palette and fooled a friend who thought Brooke's still life had been painted by Mŭhl. All artists have a beginning.

Encourage an entrepreneur's spirit. When Brooke went to dancing school in seventh grade, she and a friend decided there was a need for a company they called Worthwhile Cosmetics. They presented us with a formal request for a loan to help them launch their business: they proposed to sell little attractive baskets of essential makeup for dancing class at "reasonable prices." They were good at packaging and the company took off with most of their friends' allowances going straight to Worthwhile Cosmetics.

"Small matters win great commendation."
—FRANCIS BACON

The secret to having a close relationship with your son or daughter after they marry is to be supportive. Invite the children to come visit you but wait until you're invited to visit them. Your daughter-in-law will want the house or apartment to be at its best before you come. Don't instruct. Be busy with your own life so that you

GROWN CHILDREN

are interesting to the children. When they want advice, they'll ask.

Your daughter-in-law will have a different color sense which she will use in her choice of sheets, towels, tablecloths and napkins, wall colors, fabrics, and rugs. Don't interfere. If you want to give her a house present, offer to go with her and let her make her own selection. The colors of the bath towels, china, and pictures for the wall are far too personal for anyone else to pick out. Your way is one way and you should back off and let them figure out their own style together.

Be a supportive friend and this realtionship can thrive. Review your actions regularly so things don't become tense. Salute them as they begin their independent lives together and you will never lose them.

Be loving and kind. Bring little presents you know they'll appreciate. Never expect anything in return. Ask questions. Give them your ear. And then sit back, enjoy yourself and, most especially, them.

> "When I was at home, I was in a better place."
> —WILLIAM SHAKESPEARE

LETTING GO

Children will always be children to their parents. Don't fight it: rejoice in this truth. When you lose your parents you lose a big warm spot that is hard to give up. With both my parents dead I feel more like a parent than a child, yet a part of us wants to keep the child in us alive no matter what our age. Our parents help us to do this.

Honor is not an old-fashioned word. A child doesn't have to wait until he has his own children to understand the powerful interconnection he shares with his parents.

Every effort should be made, beginning at birth, to help a child to flower independently, to grow up and leave the nest. Birds do it, we did it, and our children must also. Let go. Encourage their solo flight. Inquire. Listen to their plans. This transition from dependence to independence can be a rich and loving one if your child feels he has your emotional support.

As I was writing yesterday I stopped and paused, looking out at a rich blue sky dotted with soft clouds. My windows had just been cleaned and this day brought ideal fresh crisp air and sparkling light. My baby daughter turned eighteen years old last week and I was daydreaming about her party, the toasts, her friends, the pink balloons. Suddenly four colorful balloons appeared—red, white, yellow, and purple, with ribbons dangling down—moving gracefully through the intense blue sky.

My trance was interrupted by a friend calling to chat. I told her about the balloons. "That's good luck," Louise told me. A friend of hers had a dream about her child's autonomy—in the dream her daughter was being carried by a balloon; she was holding on to its string and was floating. As Louise spoke, the balloons I'd spotted disappeared behind a tall apartment building and another cluster appeared. "Someone must be having a birthday party," I told Louise. "There are a lot of children up there holding on to the strings of their balloons and soaring, all part of the universe now."

GRACE NOTES

- Establish seasonal rituals with your child. The first warm day of spring, take a walk in the park. Plan a picnic for the first hot day.

- Take your children on trips. Children are never too young to absorb the enrichment of a new environment. Take lots of pictures and keep the trips alive in your minds. The children will never forget them and the knowledge of that place will stay with them forever.

- Encourage your children to collect something. They will love adding to their collection and will begin to develop their own personal style.

- Be creative in displaying your children's artwork. Buy inexpensive clear plastic frames and frame their favorite pieces. Pick a wall in the family room on which to hang them. Let them take part in arranging the masterpieces. Let your child decide what goes on the refrigerator door and what gets framed. Or buy plastic place mats that you can slip their artwork into and change them. What a great way for Mom and Dad to start the day, looking at original family art!

- Play games with your child. Checkers, jacks, Pick-up sticks. Play marbles. Children love to see parents happy.

- Hug your child.

- Have your child choose an important sports event that he would like you to attend. And then put it on your calendar.

- Encourage your child to take part in family discussions at the dinner table. Later on he will know the art of conversing.

- Let your children have a part in deciding about their space, their room. They need some personal space, too.

- Have your children help decorate your house or apartment for holidays.

- If you have a backyard, make a flower bed for your child. Buy him flower seeds, and teach him how to plant and weed and water a garden. What joy when the seed turns into a flower!

- Read, read, read books to your small children. You'll enjoy it, and it's a precious gift to instill in children a love for reading. It makes it easier for them to learn to read themselves, and helps develop imagination.

- Listen attentively to your child's thoughts.

- Make a Sunday-night ritual of making soufflés with the children.

- Rotate pictures or postcards of beautiful paintings in a child's bathroom. He can study them as he's brushing his teeth or sitting in the bathtub. It gives him a sense of taste and appreciation of beauty.

- Work on picture albums with the children. The more you talk about trips, the more they'll be remembered.

- Share with your child some of your favorite old movies. Introduce him to the Marx Brothers, *It's a Wonderful Life*, *The Sound of Music*. He'll be entertained and will be learning more of American culture.

- When a child becomes old enough, encourage him to learn how to cook something special. It will give him confidence to try new things.

- Children love to perform. The next time your children have company and they are at a loss for something to do, encourage them to put on a show. Supply them with props and be an appreciative audience. This is also a confidence booster.

- Order in Chinese food and have your children set the table with colorful bowls and chopsticks.

- Nurture creativity. If a child shows an aptitude for art, music, or sports, make sure he has an opportunity to develop it if he wishes.

- Let your child pick out her own stationery or note cards. These do not have to be expensive or engraved; thermal printing is colorful and inexpensive. This helps a child learn the courtesy of writing thank-you notes and the pleasure of correspondence.

- Instill in your children the nicety of writing a thank-you note after a party as well as thanks for a gift.

- Visit the library together often. Do not censor what your children read, and share your favorite books with them. Introduce them to the many different sections, and when they are the right age encourage them to make these trips on their own as well as with you.

- Have your children gather up the toys and clothes they don't use and accompany you when you donate these to a local thrift store or charity.

- Give your child a calligraphy set.

- Be involved in your child's school activities. This means more to your child than you may realize.

- Make Christmas and birthday gifts with them for relatives. If you've always been at a loss for ideas of this kind, grab a copy of a children's publication or a magazine or book that features articles on this sort of activity.

- Commission a portrait of your children. You will have these for yourself and for posterity. Have them painted in their element—with a favorite animal or doll, in a baseball uniform, playing "tea time." What warm memories the painting will bring as the children grow older!

- Give a serious present on a big birthday, something for life—an antique desk or an upholstered chair.

YOUR
GRACE
NOTES

Friends

Edith Wharton spoke of her friendship with Henry James: "Such a friend I found in you, an expansion of one's soul." Real friends give unconditional love. There is an easiness in the friendship because it is based on love and acceptance. Friends are mutually voluntary. Each person is free and there are no strings. We love a friend as he is. We are not out to change or correct a friend.

We get something unique and give something different to each friend. Friends can be enriching, expanding and affirming; they are good for our health. Once a friend becomes a burden, he is no longer a friend. Once strings surface, friendship dies. It is never strings that make you go and be there for a friend. You go because you want to be there.

WHAT FRIENDS ARE

I have a real need to spend my time well with friends. It is not a matter of what we do but how focused we are. Ideally we want our friends to share our intensity and passion. We want to be able to tell about the discovery of a book that has changed us, or be able to tell a powerful story. Lin Yutang wrote in his wise book

BETWEEN FRIENDS

The Importance of Living: "For unless we have passion, we have nothing . . . It is passion that is the soul of life . . . it gives us inward warmth and the rich vitality which enables us to face life cheerily."

We all have limitations of time. I have many friends I don't see more than six or eight hours a year. It is not a question of how much time we spend together but the quality of the visit. A friend told me recently that he and his wife want to make friends who will deepen their lives and enhance their growth. "We don't want to see friends just for amusement. Time is too precious."

Friends confirm us.

My experience is that two hours together in a neutral place where neither person has stress or distractions can be far more meaningful than a weekend spent together where there are interruptions and other people wanting attention. Children, spouses, the telephone, and neighbors can dilute conversation and keep you from a truly special visit.

The patterns and rhythms of our lives are in constant change and there are times when we have more time for friends than others. The arrival of a new baby can put stress on a friendship because invariably the baby steals the attention. If you are in a particularly hectic time in your life, these interruptions can leave you feeling frustrated.

I remember several years ago when a friend invited me to lunch at her country house in May. I looked forward to our visit and my expectations were high. Unfortunately, the reality was a bitter disappointment. Linda was renovating her house and there were workmen everywhere. She was distracted by the noise and confusion and kept jumping up to answer questions and the phone and the door. The only way I could be with her was to follow her around. She kept asking, "Where were we?" We were noplace! I got more nervous by the minute and kept thinking of all the work I should be doing at the office. Lunch had not been prepared. I envisioned more fussing. I took action and suggested we go to a restaurant where we could escape the bedlam. At first she said she couldn't leave. Then she felt embarrassed. But I persuaded her we'd have a much better time, because we couldn't talk in her house. Had lunch been ready ahead of time we could have sat and been together—I felt cheated because we weren't spending our time well with each other. Finally we escaped the chaos, drove to town, ordered chicken salad and iced tea, and sat face-to-face for the first time. We looked at each other and began to talk.

We have to learn to be smart about how we spend time with friends. Think how you can both be together burden-free. I've discovered I have better experiences with my friends when neither one of us is in our own home. When we are at home we fragment ourselves and without realizing it, we move away from our friend! We walk into another room, we answer the door. We give instructions. We answer questions—we answer the phone. When children are involved we always pay attention to their needs.

Visualize being at a restaurant or café with a friend having lunch. You sit together for approximately two hours. Other than ordering food, you are completely there for your friend. Those uninterrupted minutes can mean more than five times as many elsewhere.

When you do invite a friend to your house, do not answer the telephone. If no one is there to take a message, let it ring. Pretend you're out. Or put the answering machine on. Being at home should not be a trap. Be prepared. If you're serving iced tea, have it ready. If you don't know whether your friend wants coffee or tea, have the water boiling so you can quickly make either choice.

Be thoughtful of your friend's time. Guard and appreciate the precious time you have together. If you are on a leave of absence from your job or are between jobs or on vacation, chances are your friend is busier than you are. Be happy to have some good moments and then let go. Some friends we will never spend a forty-eight-hour weekend with alone. But by going to a museum exhibition together you can express the positive response of sharing and you will get more out of the exhibition than if you went alone. We have to learn to accept our friends' limits and be happy to be friends. If a friend has a lover and spends most of her free time with him, accept this. The wiser we are with the short visits with friends, the richer our friendships can become. Bumping into a friend and sharing twenty unrushed minutes together sipping espresso at a café can be rewarding and special for both of you—whereas if you both stayed for two hours, chances are one of you would be a nervous wreck because of obligations and pressures at work or home or both.

But never have friends substitute for time spent alone when you nurture yourself. If you spend excessive time being with friends and have neglected yourself and your family, you will end up being not a joy but a burden to your friends. Friends should not be used as a distraction to escape the real world. When Sally went to visit a persistent friend she ended up getting the flu. "I felt all my energy being drained out of me as she sat in her dirty apartment complaining about her ungrateful husband and daughter."

Carefully plan your time when you can nurture friends the same way you plan time alone in order to nurture yourself. If a friend calls you on the spur of the moment and wants to do something with you, don't accept just because you are free—maybe you had created that free time in order to be alone! Knowing yourself and listening to your instincts will guide you to say no when that is appropriate. When you say yes you are saying to yourself that you are ready to nurture your friend.

I'd rather risk a tiny disappointment than do something when I don't have the peace of mind to enjoy it or the grace to care about my friend's concerns. Going to a lecture or exhibition with a friend or meeting for tea is what I love to do but if I'm bogged down—for whatever reason—or if I'm desperate for some private time and would rather be with a friend another time, I need the freedom to say no.

Friends love honesty and are understanding. Inquire of a friend whether it is still convenient to meet for tea that afternoon. When you open up a question to a friend you will usually get an honest response. Friends feel under the weather sometimes too. We all get tired and discouraged. I'd rather have someone cancel a date with me than see a friend frazzled and out of sorts. Unless that person needed a sympathetic ear, I'd encourage my friend to spend some private time nurturing herself.

If you have friends who are overworked because of job responsibilities, drop a brief note to let them know you're thinking of them. Never wait for a call or letter first. Your friends will thrive knowing you are understanding of their impossible schedules. They might love to have lunch with you but just can't while they are going through their deadlines. I have several friends who disappear when they are doing something creative—acting, painting, writing—and when they have completed a body of work they surface as though nothing had happened. They don't return phone calls or answer letters, they don't RSVP invitations. Invariably they thank me for understanding ᴛ hat they have been going through. Friends never keep score. They want to be able to be themselves and be understood by their friends.

All of us are orbiting like stars in the universe. We can't have our dance card filled for the rest of our lives, we need spaces to allow for serendipity. Our friends come and go throughout our lifetime. We are always changing as we move about and grow. That's the reason why our friends change too. Samuel Johnson warned, "If a man does not make new acquaintances as he advances through life, he will soon find himself alone. A man, sir, must keep his friendships in constant repair." The friend we had in kindergarten who played in the sandbox with us probably won't be a friend for life but it doesn't make the friendship any less real. We live our lives in chapters, and we need different friends at different times. Each of us has to choose who we want most to become as an individual and our selection of friends should fit into our private goals.

Søren Kierkegaard, the Danish existentialist philosopher, made choice one of his fundamental concepts. B. Eugene Griessman, author of *The Achievement Factor*, notes: "In Kierkegaard's view, people are just faces in a crowd until they make a choice. Someone

CHANGING NEEDS

"And what he greatly thought, he nobly dared."
—*HOMER*

becomes an individual only by choosing—a mate, a religion, a political philosophy, a career. You make choices by saying no . . ." We choose by selection and rejection. We select a rose and reject a daisy, we choose Hemingway over Updike. We pick a yellow chintz over a beige tweed fabric, Hawaii over the Caribbean. The same applies with friends. We naturally reach out to others to influence us in our areas of interest. I want my friends to stretch me intellectually, to understand my longings and dreams and encourage me to embrace the future in life-enhancing ways.

Each of us has to pay attention to our special needs as we go through our growth phases; we meet these by the thoughtful choices we make. We choose a new friend and this may require saying no to another, which can be painful. We often meet friends by chance, but by the conscious choice they meet our current needs and desires. We change and so do our friends. As we grow more mature and a little wiser, we look for friends who reinforce what is positive in our lives. If we eventually find we can't share this optimistic energy and spirit reciprocally, we choose other friends. Each friend should add a powerful dimension of pleasure, intimacy, and grace. "Each friend represents a world in us, a world possibly not born until they arrive, and it is only by this meeting that a new world is born," Anaïs Nin, the diarist, explains.

"Time," said Gloria Steinem, "is all there is." Time is so precious, and friends need unhurried time. With a friend we set aside our busy-ness, sharing the meaning behind all our activities, pausing and reflecting, becoming the person we most want to be. I enjoy being both strong and vulnerable with a friend and want to try to understand what their desires are too. In bad times I want us to be there for each other physically and spiritually.

What are your personal wishes for a friend? Maybe you want an "encourager," someone who will listen to you and cheer you along. Maybe you want a friend who helps you on your spiritual journey, or one who stimulates your mind and intensifies life's possibilities for you. Friends are deliciously selfish. We bring these chosen people into our private interior lives because subconsciously

"Self-love . . . is not so vile a sin As self-neglecting."
—*WILLIAM SHAKESPEARE*

"Each friend represents a world in us."
—*ANAÏS NIN*

we believe we have something positive and powerful to give each other.

"Friendship is the marriage of the soul," Voltaire wrote.

I think of close friends as soul mates—friends we love and trust so implicitly that we want to think out loud with them. Listening and talking, communicating, sharing silences are the main event. When we are together, whether sitting on a terrace or at an attractive restaurant, the conversation will pick up where it left off last time.

Usually we have a handful of close, nurturing friends at a time. Eugene Kennedy says, "The real test of friendship is: Can you literally do nothing with the other person? Can you enjoy being together those moments of life that are utterly simple? They are the moments that people look back on at the end of life and number as their most sacred experiences. . . . If you find you can't be with someone unless you're doing something together—skiing, going to a play, in other words, a third thing to which you both direct your attention—then that person may not be as good a friend as you think." What I am most attracted to in my friends is their spirit: people who love life, who are passionate, who take risks to live fully, who are sensitive to feelings and idiosyncrasies, who have a real need to share this goodness with me. Having and being a friend means wanting only the best for each other, and the bond allows each of you to grow and flower to his fullest capacity. Some of our best friends we met, I believe, by fate. This friendship is the deepest life offers you. A friendship can go on and grow as far as you'll allow it to. When we have someone who encourages us to be ourselves, who loves us as we are, we have an incomparable treasure.

"The most I can do for my friend is simply to be his friend."
—HENRY DAVID THOREAU

Make a real effort to find times to be alone together with a best friend. I flew out to Illinois this winter to see my oldest friend, and we sat at her kitchen table for three hours sipping Virgin Marys,

189

then we had coffee after lunch. The phone was off the hook and we had privacy so we could feel comfortable discussing tough subjects without fear of being overheard, misunderstood, judged, or interrupted. I flew back to New York satisfied and happy because we'd had a meaningful private time together, the first in too many years. Cicero believed, "Friendship makes prosperity brighter, while it lightens adversity by sharing its griefs and anxieties."

A "THIRD LOG"

Our lives are structured and we have so much we want to do. Having a mutual interest, project, or talent helps to bring you together with friends in a meaningful way. My term for this is a "third log." I think of my camp days as a child and how vital the third log was to make a campfire. Friends allow us to share certain parts of our lives without interfering with our overall sense of privacy and innate need for solitude. When you share an event—a play, a party, a museum, concert, auction, movie, or sports event—with a friend, you share companionship while doing something of mutual delight. A "third log" shared with friends can be a life-enhancing, happy time. You want to do certain things anyway and so being with a friend you know enjoys the same kind of experience expands your pleasure without your having to spend any extra time.

For instance, I have two friends who have season tickets to the New York Philharmonic and they know months in advance they will share a mutually enjoyable evening of music together. Other friends have season tickets to the Shakespeare festival so they plan a little supper together before the theater in order to catch up and they stop for cappuccino afterward to discuss the play. This event is firm and because they have the pleasure of anticipation, their meetings are always special. Other close friends adore eating in good restaurants and plan four dinners a year where they savor each other's company and a memorable meal.

Maybe you have a tennis friend you meet once a week and can

"Friendship needs a certain parallelism of life, a community of thought."
—HENRY ADAMS

enjoy playing and conversing with. I have friends who exercise together. Two afternoons a week Karen and Sarah meet, alternating apartments, and they play favorite tapes and work out. Afterward they sit at the kitchen table and banter, discussing anything from what they'll plan for dinner to a book they're reading to world affairs. Having a regular date is a good way to be sure you get time to be with each other.

Carol and Betsy live far apart so they keep in touch by mail. Carol lives in a small town in North Carolina and loves to pull up a chair and visit with Betsy, who lives in New Jersey. She pulls her chair to the typewriter and carries on a conversation on paper. Betsy returns the correspondence in a similar chatty style, only she prefers sitting in a comfortable chair and writing in longhand on pale blue paper attached to a clipboard. Once a year they see each other. They both decide where they want to go for a visit. One year it was Washington in April to see the cherry blossoms, another year it was Nantucket in late spring before the tourists descended. Neither of them has much money so they've developed a travel fund where they save their change and once a month they put it in rolls, go to the bank, deposit it in a savings account, and anticipate their trip.

One of my friends has developed the ritual of calling me every Saturday morning. Lindsay knows exactly where I am at 10:30 A.M. Saturdays. I'm in bed! She calls no matter where she is, and whenever she can't reach me she assumes I'm on an exotic trip somewhere and forgot to tell her. We have kept up this Saturday phone friendship over several years and I look forward to my phone call enormously. The calls I receive at the office are business-related and I'm usually in a room with other people. It is never the same when you just want to chat as when you have some unpressured free time.

Develop rituals with friends.

I have a friend who lives one block away and we share hand-delivered notes. We select pretty cards from museums or card stores, and we share our feelings and immediate activities. There is a special magical quality to these hand-delivered notes because they arrive at odd, unexpected times, at isolated moments when the regular mail doesn't come—early morning or Sunday afternoon. I keep her latest note on my white wicker writing table in my bedroom and when the spirit moves me I sit down and answer it with a pretty card. This note-exchanging ritual is one I treasure participating in, and when I actually see my friend we are freshly caught up on each other's lives.

I have a friend who calls and offers me a choice of three dates to go to the theater. Friends know better than to say, "We must get together." Act. Make definite dates. Never be hurt if a busy friend doesn't have a free moment for several weeks. Enjoy anticipating a future date.

Make plans. Sprinkle friendship dates throughout your business calendar. Keep a good balance between work and taking time out to be with friends.

Make a date with your flower-loving friend to go to the Botanical Gardens in early spring and prepare an elegant picnic so that you can sit on a pretty quilt in an attractive setting and enjoy sharing the beauty.

If you have a friend who travels a great deal, check in regularly so you know the schedule for several weeks and try to make a date to talk on the phone so you can set something up between trips.

When you read about special exhibitions in the newspaper, whether it's a Cecil Beaton retrospective or Cezanne's drawings at the art museum, think of a particular friend you'd like to go see the exhibit with, pick up the phone, give times and dates, and mutually set a time and place to meet.

The pioneer women of America socialized over their quilting bees, their church work, their cooking at barn raisings—they were together for a purpose and they enjoyed themselves and their companionship. We tend to have more time to develop close friendships when we have shared common experiences and interests—photography, art, music or dance, writing, designing, figure skating, or discussing good literature.

All of us at some time in our lives will have a "surprise" friend—we will be "surprised by joy," as C. S. Lewis wrote. Someone will come along and be totally incongruous, out of our daily realm, who adds spice, adventure, vitality, and completeness to our life. Let this person who seems so different from you stretch your imagination. My surprise friends are different not only from me but from each other. Their common denominator is that they are having fun with their lives, they love what they are doing.

I enjoy the story of how Claude Monet got started painting. As a young man he worked in a paint store near Normandy. Eugène Boudin would come in to buy his paint supplies and was waited on by young Claude. Eugène told Claude he painted out-of-doors at the beaches in Normandy and suggested that Claude join him sometime when he was off from work. And that's exactly what Monet did and how he started painting.

A struggling young writer meets a senior editor at *Reader's Digest* at a poolside dance and they hit it off. A cancer doctor meets a designer at a benefit. A restaurant owner enjoys one of his regular customers. These people are in our lives for a purpose—to expand us, shake us up, make us more aware of areas of interest and parts of the world that will help us to be more whole. Embrace these surprise friends. You will invariably be "surprised by joy." Who do you know now that you would like as your surprise friend? In your own way you should convey your special warmth and friendship toward this person because this spark is never one-sided. Someone has to make the first move.

We would all benefit if we had a wise and trusted counselor to look up to and try to emulate. We've all had a favorite teacher or an excellent, understanding boss, or someone in our neighborhood

A SURPRISE FRIEND

Friendship affirms life.

MENTOR

193

when we were growing up who took a special interest in us and taught us truths through example. This mentor relationship is special. Almost always there is a considerable age difference between the mentor and the protégée. A good mentor is a trainer, someone who believes in the person and teaches, supports, and instructs not only about a profession or a career, but about life. I've been blessed with four powerful mentors. My first was my art teacher, Phyl Gardner, and she was responsible for my deciding to go directly to art school after I graduated from high school. That decision led to my meeting Mrs. Brown, whose lecture I attended, and I set my sights on working for her and her great firm. My third mentor, John Coburn, an old friend of my aunt Betty Johns, became my minister and my spiritual guide. My fourth was a senior editor from *Reader's Digest* who recognized my longing to become a writer.

A mentor doesn't have to do anything extra in order to be a positive influence and guide for a younger protégée. Many people in positions of authority enjoy passing on the wisdom they were fortunate to learn over the years from other wise and trusted people. Sometimes a protégée learns from observation and sharing views because her mentor makes himself available.

Mentors, like all good teachers, instinctively know when they are no longer needed for instruction and teaching, and the relationship, in time, becomes one of lasting friendship and mutual respect. A mentor must let the protégée go, become independent, and gain self-confidence through self-reliance. A mentor will always take great pride in the accomplishments and successes of someone they have spent time nurturing. Phyl Gardner told me that if she was able to spark one student every few years she considered herself lucky. So there is an element of luck involved, being at the right place at the right time when mentor and protégée are mutually receptive to each other. A protégée benefits by example. No matter how different her own style becomes, there are certain fundamental disciplines, once observed, that tend to last a lifetime. Eventually the relationship, like that of parent and child, must change: the thoughtful mentor kicks the protégée out of the nest to fly alone, never losing the deep satisfaction and sense of pride. Loss is an essential element in all such relationships and when we do things right, letting go gracefully is a kindness and another loving lesson to be observed. The relationship shifts from that of teacher-student to one of mutual admiration. An English major at Wellesley College became a secretary and protégée of a senior editor at a major publishing house and after two years was advised to "go be an assistant editor. You can no longer be my secretary." Real mentors are never selfish. As a struggling young writer I was fortunate to have been nursed along by a mentor who finally left me to think on my own: Bob wrote to me once I was a published author and, in a very sincere way, said good-bye. "I only want to read your work once it's in print. You're an author now. Knock them dead. Good luck." I was left to my own resources. As I continue to publish I always sense it pleases my mentor to know his time and guidance weren't wasted.

Of my mentors, one has died and the other three have stopped teaching me. Collectively they have helped me to be where I am now. In turn, I try to be a mentor to young, talented women starting out in the field of design. I enjoy the sense of continuity. All of us should be open to this form of friendship and reach out and nurture someone who is searching for direction, for something to become passionate about, for inspiration, and for someone to look up to for guidance. Often a young person just needs to observe you. Make yourself available. Invite a protégée to a museum exhibition or a fashion show, a reception at your house, or any event you enjoy. This availability and exposure is invaluable. A protégée will be honored to be included and will stretch you to experience these events from a fresh viewpoint.

You may find that you have a protégée who eventually surpasses you. You opened up to this younger person and genuinely tried to help because you believed you could make a difference. Time passes. We have to love and let go. We can be proud to know we had a hand in someone's success. What satisfaction we can feel knowing we are a part of the continuity of caring and have influenced someone worthy in a positive way!

FRIENDS OF A DIFFERENT SEX

"Life is too short to neglect any opportunities."
—BROOKE STODDARD

I find it essential to my happiness to have male friends. I would feel only half alive without them. Many of the men are married and their spouses usually prefer keeping their husbands to themselves. But it is well worth the effort to have opposite-sex friends. They are so wonderful because they give you a different perspective. They are the other half of your understanding. When you have a sister-like or brother-like friendship, a relationship that is natural and open, you are allowed to be fully yourself without fear of embarrassment or rejection.

Disregard traditional taboos. Women should feel free to be seen with their male friends without fear of damaging their reputation. Actions speak for us. Self-confidence and good intentions allow you to enjoy yourself. Nurture a few opposite-sex friends if they vitalize your life and bring you joy. If I act in a trustworthy manner I expect my husband, who loves me and respects me, to be secure enough himself so that I am free to expand my world of understanding by having a few male friends.

Many opposite-sex friendships are possible only when two couples see each other together. If that works, accept the boundaries. But it's best to find a workable way to have opposite-sex friends.

"Most friendships begin with a compliment."
—PETER MEGARGEE BROWN

If you have friends of the opposite sex, remain open and try not to let anyone interfere. If I want to be alone with a male friend in order to have a meaningful one-on-one exchange, I tell Peter whom I'm meeting and where. He is happy for me. Most of my male friends are professional friends so it would be inappropriate for Peter to be included. Peter, in turn, enjoys friendships with his female clients and meets with them informally over lunch after a meeting. What I don't approve of is being sneaky and seeing someone behind a partner's back.

We want to share all our different kinds of friends and celebrate them. It is at parties that our friends are free to meet our other friends in a cheerful atmosphere.

What is fun is planning a party and inviting a variety of friends so that you feel you are creating a good mix. Don't worry about who knows whom. Invariably your friends open up and find all sorts of common interests. You are the host or hostess and everyone you invite is a friend of yours. Have tea at your apartment or house. Have a reception in honor of a friend who had just received a promotion or has done something deserving of recognition. Have a few friends over for breakfast before the rest of the world is up. If you have a friend who is an artist and you belive in his or her work, arrange to have other friends come to a showing where you live.

Connecting friend to friend is one of the real joys of entertaining. Whenever possible, when you are having a sit-down dinner party, have place cards so a guest can refer to his or her dinner partner by name. "Good manners is the art of making those people easy with whom we converse. Whoever makes the fewest persons uneasy is the best bred in the company," claimed Jonathan Swift in 1720 in his "A Treatise on Good Manners and Good Breeding."

When you are introduced to a stranger, be sure you hear his name. When we are nervous we have to concentrate in order to be good listeners. If you don't hear the name and register it properly, ask. Nothing is more important than one's name, at least to the person. Make an association. For instance, you meet a man at a party whose first name is Tom. Think of Tom Wolfe and you'll never forget his name. Throughout the evening when you see him you can look him in the eye and refer to him by name as you introduce him to others. Next, you meet Mary. Think of Mary Martin. You'll always be able to remember Mary. Play a game with yourself and challenge yourself to remember as many names as possible.

ENTERTAINING FRIENDS

"Love each other to a crisp."
—ALEXANDRA BRANDON STODDARD

197

Studies on memory have proved that focus is essential and age is not a necessary factor in memory loss. Once you get a name right, introduce Tom or Mary to others right away. Say the name under your breath three times and then make the association with Tom Wolfe or Mary Martin. Chances are you will have put the name in safekeeping in your memory bank.

When you move around at a party and introduce yourself to one or two people are who mingling in the group, immediately shake hands with those you haven't met and introduce yourself. Introduce to the other people you've just met someone you've just introduced yourself to. When you have eye contact and introduce yourself right away, no one has to apologize for forgetting your name.

If you are the host or hostess and take guests around the room introducing them to the crowd, try to say a word or two about your friends so when the guests are on their own they can mingle and be free to start a conversation. "So, you're in the art world. Tell me, what is your specialty?" The ice is broken.

Gather a wide variety of your friends. You are the common thread. You want your friends to meet and get to know one another. Because so many of our friends we've met through other friends, the friendship chain has many tender links and a history. The ripple effect will always exist even when you and I are not aware of it. Ask a guest, "How do you know our hostess?" and you will usually hear an interesting story.

Clare Boothe Luce would sit at a dinner party and pose well-honed questions, such as asking a cancer surgeon if there had been any significant breakthroughs in curing cancer in the past ten years. Her questions were direct and riveting and she was such an attentive listener that she won the hearts of all her dinner partners. In our complex society, asking the right questions at the right time can be crucial in obtaining information we need to carry on our side of the conversation. Dialogue becomes interesting, energetic communication. My husband wrote a book entitled *The Art of Questioning* which has many useful maxims to help us acquire information.

Asking good questions *is* an art and it can be learned. Match that with an equally necessary talent, giving your full attention to the one talking, and you will improve your chances to make and keep friends.

"Love thy neighbor as thyself," the Bible tells us. But I believe   NEIGHBORS
Robert Frost was right when he said in his poem "Mending Wall"
that "good fences make good neighbors." He was also right, in the
same poem, when he advised, "Before I built a wall I'd ask to know
what I was walling in or walling out." We don't choose the family
who moves into the house or apartment next door; these are people
fate has given to us. I firmly believe we should be courteous and
polite to our neighbors and let them know we will be a friend-in-
need. However, as the world's problems tend to crush in on us and
our home is our only private world of retreat, it is wise to maintain
your privacy by not allowing your neighbors to interfere with your
peace, privacy, and happiness. Good manners make for excellent
neighbors.

As an interior designer I've heard many uplifting, happy stories
about neighbors, and I've also heard some pretty sad ones. One
neighbor couldn't stand the noise of her neighbor's renovation and
arranged for a work stoppage "because the noise was driving her
insane." Her own apartment had been renovated far more exten-
sively two years before, but she soon developed amnesia and other
people's noise was unacceptable.

Many neighbors are instinctively thoughtful and care about the
welfare of those nearby. A bachelor client received a package from
his immediate neighbor the day he was having a huge party with
a note: "Dear Ed, If you want to move some of your furniture into
our apartment or need extra ice or glasses, feel free to use our
apartment as a resource. Please use our kitchen, including the ovens
and microwave, as needed. I will be home all morning if you want
to talk. Have a super party. Sally and I will see you tonight." The

present wasn't opened until after the party when all the guests were gone. A small green rectangular piece of needlework with a loop to put over a doorknob with the words "My Neighbors are Perfect" was resting inside a silver-colored box. Ed has this inside his dressing-room door to remind himself how perfect *his* neighbors are.

Another client had a neighbor whose wife was sick in bed with cancer. Without any formal plan to help, neighbors brought "I care" packages of food because the wife was too weak to cook and there were three teenage children at home. The food packages kept coming and through word of mouth neighbors felt gratified their gestures were helpful.

A bachelor was going crazy when his kitchen was being renovated because they had disconnected his ice machine and refrigerator so he couldn't have a refreshing drink after work. When he was complaining to his neighbors at a supper party he was handed an extra key to their apartment so he could get himself some ice each night on his way home from work. I remember when our appliances were being painted, not only did the kitchen smell awful but we had no use of the appliances. A neighbor's daughter brought us an ice-packed container full of cooked shrimp and lemons.

Clients who live in the same building share folding chairs. They each store half the chairs and after eleven years they have never had a meeting or dinner party at the same time. They check in with each other!

Being polite and showing courtesy always has its rewards. If you're planning a noisy party, warn your neighbors ahead of time. If you feel it's appropriate, invite them to stop by. The golden rule works wonders. If the decisions you make will affect your neighbors, drop them a note and arrange for a meeting to discuss it. We all hate to be taken advantage of and we don't appreciate surprises. If you are planning to build a swimming pool it is a kindess to let your neighbors know well ahead of the bulldozing in case they want to dirtproof their house.

Loud music or television, late wild parties, fighting—it is usually some noise violation that irritates neighbors.

> "Love thy neighbour
> as thyself."
> —*LEVITICUS*

If your neighbors are new to your neighborhood it is a kind gesture to introduce them to some of your friends and help them learn what services are best in the community. If you find you've established a rapport with your neighbors and you trust them implicitly, let them know when you will be away. If something strange happens to your house when you aren't there, they can call the police. I heard about a family who went off on a two-week holiday, and while they were gone a huge moving van arrived. Four men broke into the house and removed everything except the curtains while the neighbors all watched. "I didn't know the Smiths were moving. I wonder who bought their house. Who will our new neighbors be?" The only problem was, the Smiths weren't moving and this was a carefully planned wipe-out robbery. I heard another story of a lady going to the hairdresser before leaving for a European vacation; she was overheard bragging about her big month's trip. The robbers knew they had lots of time and posed as people doing cabinetry work in the house. Some of the finer antiques were removed from the house "because they needed to be repaired in the shop." All the paintings, jewelry, and silver were placed inside the antiques that left the house. Large paintings were strapped to large tables and hidden by the padded blankets. Everything was meticulously put into the truck over a two-week period. A knowing neighbor could have done something. Virtually everything of value was gone and there were no fingerprints left behind because the professional robbers wore gloves while inside the house.

Relations

Relatives are an extension of our immediate family and they give us a secondary support system. Families can provide continuity, linking us with our past and adding depths of diversity to our lives.

"Life is born out of force and denial at the hand's of one's intimates," says Vivian Gornick in her article "The World and Our Mothers" (*New York Times Book Review*, November 22, 1987).

Enjoy the luxury of time, a place, and loved ones.

We can learn from one another and share the common thread of our family ties, reaching out in loving, positive ways to our extended family. Just knowing that you have a loving family can help you adapt. We will always be our parents' children and our children will always be ours, but we grow through different kinds of dependency and intensity.

The key to successful relations with your relatives is to act in a loving manner by loving yourself and them on your own terms. In the novel *The Unlit Lamp* by Radclyffe Hall (author of *The Well of Loneliness*), Mary cries out to her brave, spirited fourteen-year-old daughter Joan, "Don't leave me, darling. You're all I have in the world. Without you I'll die." The mother sounds like a dependent child in need of security. Parents shouldn't depend on their children for wholeness. Love doesn't work that way. Joan's life is destroyed because she is too afraid to leave her needy mother.

Families like to sit around the table and pass on endless stories, revealing the essence of the past. By holding on to memories of the good old days as well as tales of hardship and suffering, valuable lessons are absorbed. We may be told a story of our grandfather working in a coal factory so that we could go to college. Family history matters: it connects us and enriches us.

Usually we have one parent who is strong and dominating. My mother clearly ran our family.

MOTHER

Of all the intimacies, no relationship will ever have as many consequences as our connection with our mother. This century has enlarged our understanding about the struggle and the conflicts of separating from our mother. In *The Unlit Lamp* Joan's tutor Elizabeth urges her to leave her mother and "come live with me in London. You'll go to Cambridge, become a doctor, become anything you want. If you don't get away from here you'll not have life." Joan stays and her "feelings for her mother drag her down, making her vulnerable, guilty and full of pity."

Just as parents should not expect their children to complete them, children, once grown up, must find a way to break with their childhood. Other people can love and nurture us, but all of us have only one mother. This physical and psychological closeness causes an intensely emotional relationship. In our appreciation of the sacrifices our mother has made on our behalf, we tie up a great deal of our energy trying to be worthy and accepted positively. We want our mother to be proud of us. This feeling can continue even after our mother dies.

If we get along well with our mother, it is largely due to love and acceptance. We can't live the same life as our mother—if we tried, it would be settling down into an unlived life. Because our mother gave us unqualified love when we were younger and we loved our mother in much the same way, this separation is rarely an easy transition. As a parent, I understand my need to have the girls love me even when they don't agree with me. When they accept me and don't try to change me then there can be real sharing and joy. Mothers, as well as children I've discovered, are starved for unqualified love, and this must be reciprocal.

I've spoken with several women my age who have maintained a relationship with their mothers that is based largely on respect, loyalty, caring, and gratitude rather than intimacy and deep, abiding love. Accept this.

Our mothers have spent most of their time trying to teach us, correct us, improve us, equip us in every way to meet future challenges. Now, as adults, we look at our teacher and want her to give us a good grade, and tell us how wonderful we are! We will always seek our mother's approval, no matter what our age.

As a child of an extremely strong mother, I felt her love and affection for me throughout my childhood even though she was strict. A month before my mother died, I gave a two-day design seminar at the University of California at San Diego. I sent an invitation to her in the hospital. The next time I went to visit her, the fold-out invitation poster was up on the wall of her hospital room for everyone to see. I'd pass nurses in the hall and they knew about the seminar. It was especially touching because I'd had enough success and interesting design assignments before she died that she had a real sense she had led the way for my design career.

If you have a mother in ill health, the best thing you can do for her is to try to live as normal a life as possible so she can delight in you, be proud of you, and feel the tremendous satisfaction that she has done a good job raising you.

I met a mother of three daughters recently who gave my last book, *Living a Beautiful Life*, to each one—a minister, a sheep raiser, and an accountant. "They're all so different and so very special because of it." Our mothers try to prepare us for a happy life, and it is our job to be mature enough to make choices that will lead to our own self-fulfillment as well as self-sufficiency.

I've always thought it would be fun to raise my daughters as though I were their grandmother. I could have all the fun and never be stuck with the nitty-gritty, day-to-day demands, the real-life drama of their growing up. In some ways I did act a bit like a young grandmother. I just enjoyed being with Alexandra and Brooke and was not nervous or afraid of the responsibility. It all seemed natural to me. Is there anything more endearing than to observe the pride grandparents take in their grandchildren? I raised the girls with the pride of a grandmother.

Grandparents always have been magical for grandchildren. Children see them as wise men and women of long experience who are kind and fun to be with. Many grandparents know how to do things with their hands because they grew up in an era when people did more physical labor; they knew a world without television, fast food, and computer mania. Children today especially look up to their grandmothers who stayed home all day to be "real" mothers, making sure everyone was happy.

Sit down with any grandmother and she will admit her deep concern for the way her grandchildren are being raised today—she'll say parents just aren't spending enough time with their children. One troubled grandmother of four told me over tea, "I realize more than ever that every word, tone, gesture, event, builds toward the child's future, their attitude, their whole character. You can't tell me a day-care center will do as good a job as a loving mother. So, while my daughter is out in the work force, I spend most of my free time with her children." A writer friend from Birmingham, Alabama, was raised on a farm in Mississippi and spent most of her childhood being raised by her grandmother. Her mother worked on local political issues. Mary Lee has fond memories of the gentle pace of life and her grandmother's nurturing manner.

We all know we can't go back to the horse-and-buggy days. We can't even raise our children the way we were raised by our parents. But we can enjoy doing things with our children when we

GRAND-
PARENTS

"Be not afraid of greatness: some are born great, some achieve greatness, and some have greatness thrust upon 'em."
—WILLIAM SHAKESPEARE

aren't under pressure and in a hurry. Mary Lee remembers thirty years later how her grandmother brushed her long straight brown hair and then how she enjoyed the ritual of having her hair braided. How often do we foolishly forget how important those moments can be? We can rake leaves together, cook together, go for walks together, and enjoy unhurried rituals. We can bake and can vegetables and make grape jelly together. Many children grow up today and don't experience good smells coming from their own kitchen. We can learn from our grandparents' wisdom, values, and character. Our children need to spend time with their grandparents so they understand firsthand about the blessings of unhurried time and loving action.

Once a year The Spence School has a day they devote to grandparents, and my mother wouldn't have missed coming and participating. She loved her role as a grandparent and became extremely attached to the girls. I could tell how much happiness they brought her by her enthusiasm and energy when she'd spend time with them. She thought they were extraordinary and I never remember a negative comment coming from her lips about my daughters. She loved to teach them and because she was spared the daily worries all parents experience, her joy wasn't tempered by fear. She actually enjoyed being a grandmother more than a mother because "the fear element" that goes with being a concerned parent was largely eliminated. They were my responsibility, her pride and joy.

Peter and I have a friend who started an organization called "Adopt a Grandparent." Children are blessed when they have grandparents. If you want to have children and can't conceive, you can adopt a child. Our friend decided that if you want a grandparent for yourself or your children you should also be able to adopt one!

Everyone wins when grandparents are active in the appreciation of their grandchildren. They understand life's transience and can reinforce the continuity of love and spiritual values through the wisdom gained by experience. Grandparents force us to pause and reflect on the pleasures of a more reasonable, less hectic pace. They

"The supreme happiness of life is the conviction that we are loved."
—*VICTOR HUGO*

don't see any virtue in faster and more; they value quality, character, and goodness.

A federal judge and his second wife have nine grandchildren between them, many at colleges dotted across the country. They now spend their vacations planning trips where they can visit their grandchildren. Mildred will call a grandchild and say, "We're going to be nearby and would love to take you and your friends out to dinner." "Then," she told me with a chuckle, "when everything is set up, we come! A very nice arrangement for us, that's for sure." Another couple I know living in Hawaii came to New England this year to see the fall foliage and managed to see twelve of their nineteen grandchildren!

Gertrude Stein reminded us, "We are always the same age inside." Having grandchildren to nurture and support doesn't make grandparents feel old; on the contrary, it helps them forget their age. Youth always resuscitates our spirits. "Living," said Anaïs Nin, "never wore one out so much as the effort not to live."

Children can make grandparents feel needed and useful, especially those living by themselves. Plan regular visits to see your grandchildren. Make yourself available. The rewards will more than make up for the effort. Write short notes to them and have little gifts when they visit. Send cookies and cheese through the mail. A college senior told me with tears in her eyes that her grandfather gave her a twenty-dollar bill and said, "Get an ice cream at the airport and keep the change." Chocolate, an African violet, some colorful postcards from your travels, stamps, a picture book, a little financial sweetener. Celebrate grandparenting by being involved.

"Gratitude is a fruit of great cultivation."
—SAMUEL JOHNSON

COUSINS

Cousins can act as close friends we didn't select. When we are thrown together with our cousins at a family reunion we can actually be surprised by how much we really enjoy getting to know them and how much fun it is to share ourselves.

My cousin Betty went around the world with me thirty years

ago and returned after the three-month trip to marry her high school sweetheart. They have raised a family and have a hapy life together. On the trip we fixed her up with a medical student from Burma who went to Stanford University and who had planned to go back to Rangoon to work as a surgeon at the hospital. We felt this would be a colorful life for Betty and she did too! But once home, Betty went right back to Ted. She's happy and doesn't judge me for living in New York City, raising children here, being a working mother— she accepts me.

A SPECIAL AUNT

My father's older sister was my favorite aunt. Aunt Betty made a real effort to get to know her three oldest nieces. She took us around the world when we were teenagers. We had so much fun riding elephants together in India, dressing in colorful silk saris, and reminiscing about home. Betty was Auntie Mame—eccentric, fun to be with, opinionated and brilliant, she refused to put up with fools. The world was her back porch. Betty would have made a wonderful mother because she encouraged us to live with vitality, courage and diversity. As an international social worker she had very little money but she lived more fully than many of our West-port, Connecticut, neighbors; they tended to accumulate things, rather than life-enriching experiences. She loved exposing us to the real world and exemplified Henry James's philosophy that one should "Live all you can; it's a mistake not to." She wanted us to see all corners of the world and explore all the possibilities open to us. She didn't understand limits, only opportunities. She never judged us or our parents, but she wanted to expose us to things we probably wouldn't experience otherwise, like riding on a third-class train from New Delhi to Agra to see the Taj Mahal. Aunt Betty was alone and free and could do special, exciting things because she had no permanent attachments or family obligations. Yet I'm sure we all know a single aunt who doesn't make this grand gesture for her nieces.

When we came back from our three months away I lived with her near Union Theological Seminary in New York City during my first year at art school. My daybed was in her study and several mornings a week I'd awake to the smell of brownies. Betty made brownies at 5 A.M. and sent them in tins to her nieces and nephews who were away at boarding school and college. Once I was awake (and relishing the smell of chocolate), she'd feel free to come into her study to attack her pile of correspondence. I enjoyed her companionship and sensed she adored having me curled up under the covers in her daybed. As I read I observed her morning habits. This remarkable woman corresponded with over five hundred people around the world and I witnessed her outpouring of energy and encouragement to her family, parents, friends, colleagues. She made an effort to give news and share insights in each communication. I saw the enormous pleasure she derived from writing these daily letters. Many of them were quite long because she'd get carried away in the pleasure of the process. She had visitors from all over the world and living with her was similar to staying at a United Nations camp.

The night before Aunt Betty died, she called me. It was a muggy night in August and we'd just driven in from Connecticut with the girls in heavy Sunday-night traffic. We were hot, tired, and out of sorts. Betty likes an immediate update—a real slice of what's going on here and now in your life. She insisted I tell her what I had planned for dinner. Had I set a pretty table? How were the girls doing with their swimming lessons? How was my tennis? She confirmed our lunch date for Tuesday. She even asked me how my writing was coming along. When I told her I found it difficult to find time to write she admonished me, "Sandie, your book is important. Stick with it. As soon as the girls go to sleep, write before your own dinner." The next morning she was giving a speech at the UN and was rushed to the hospital—she had had a heart attack. I learned later I was one of thirty-two family members she had called that Sunday evening—we all received a similar pep talk.

Because of her example I realize how important it is to mark

"What his heart thinks his tongue speaks."
—WILLIAM SHAKESPEARE

209

your calendar every other week to call a favorite aunt. Give your local florist a standing order, so something will always be in bloom, for a flowering plant to be delivered to your aunt. When you think of a favorite uncle, send him a silly card or a note. Have extra copies of pictures taken from parties or weekend outings and send a few along to an aunt or uncle. Always label the people and give dates on the back. Clip out articles that interest you and send them in brightly colored envelopes purchased at a stationery store. Make a tape of your activities and thoughts and send it with a note, "Thinking of You." Make a video of your children. Send invitations to your parties and send along information about your activities so your relatives can keep up with you. Remember, they are proud of you so you should share your activities and successes. Invite a favorite aunt to come to a dinner party early and let her help whip cream or make a sauce for the dessert.

GRACE
NOTES

- Tell one friend how wonderful another friend is and then bring them together for tea at your house.

- Get a family portrait taken in black and white and one in color. Frame some for yourself and send copies to relatives.

- When a friend or relative wears a flattering dress or suit, give a compliment.

- Associate certain relatives with their interests. Send Aunt Susie, the gardener, a pansy card. When you hear a joke, jot it on a postcard and send it to Mary, who appreciates a good laugh.

- Experiment with different-scented candles and potpourri. Buy extra and make a selection for a friend or neighbor.

- Collect small, pretty boxes so you can give seashells or a few colorful marbles to a friend.

- When relatives come to visit, have them leave with a package of goodies—make an "I care" package for them and hand it to them when they leave.

- The next time you go to a museum, buy several copies of your favorite postcards and make a few sets tied in ribbon to give away to friends. If you have a friend who has to go to the hospital, this is an ideal gift because the cards don't take up space and can be admired even when someone is lying down.

- The next time you hear a good joke, pick up the phone and tell a friend.

- Have a family sports meet. Make divisions by age, from youngest to oldest. Even babies can participate in crawling races or "silliest faces" competition, nursery schoolers in end-to-end newspaper relays, grandparents in croquet or funniest family anecdotes or joke telling.

- Think of all children as national treasures.

- "Superior people never make long visits." (Marianne Moore, American poet)

- Never worry what other people think because it doesn't matter. What they think will change and what you think will change. That's life. Be yourself.

- Visualize a garden. Each flower represents a friend. Always have a fresh flower on your desk. It will help you to think of your friends.

- Parents, give more space to grown children. They need to find their own identity, and remember they are struggling.

- When writing a child at college, sign your letter in code—say Pierre instead of Mom. It will make your daughter laugh and she can pretend she got a love letter from an admirer.

- Treat your friend to a manicure or a pedicure. If you have a friend who resists regular exercise, treat her to one of your exercise classes. She might get hooked.

- Bring a favorite flower when you meet a friend, for her hair, or his buttonhole.

- Every morning write at least one handwritten note thanking someone for benefits received the day or week before.

- If you have a favorite older aunt or grandfather who has been eager to visit a place like Williamsburg or Thomas Jefferson's home, Monticello, go with them. The trip will mean so much to both of you.

- Take pictures at a friend's party, have prints made of all the guests and send them along with a little note.

- Bring your own note cards to the flower shop so your own handwriting is on the greeting. Whenever possible, select your own flowers or plant you send as a gift. It makes a difference.

- When you discover a good Bordeaux or Brie or corn pickle relish, buy extra to pass on to friends.

- When a friend goes into a new business, have a cocktail reception to introduce him to your friends.

- Jot down on a piece of paper the names of all your family members and keep them in your Filofax. Glance at your list from time to time and know you are not alone.

- Bring a friend to a service at a synagogue or church. Introduce your friend to the worshipers.

- Put together a photo album for your sibling with pictures of him or her over the years. Gather pictures from different relatives and get copies made. Add souvenirs and mementoes, and write a line or two, something to giggle at, under the photographs. Tie the whole package with a ribbon and present it on their birthday.

- Call your host or hostess the next morning and say "thank you." Or drop a brief note in the mail. You won't regret your effort.

- Brush up on an artist, an author, a poet, a gardener. Share your subject with a friend gracefully.

- Never take your eyes off the person you are with until he or she does. Let an interruption not be caused by you. Darting your eyes is insulting.

- Be generous of spirit. Life on earth is transitory. It is better to live rich and die poor than the other way around. Being generous focuses on your self-worth, not your net worth.

- Call a stepchild and make a lunch date for two. Be early and ask questions about his plans and his dreams.

- When you see a small item that you think suits a friend, buy it and send it. The ceramic soap dish your friend admired which is now on sale, a paperback book you know he'll enjoy—make it a surprise gift.

- Clip magazine and newspaper articles you think will be of particular interest and send them.

- Save the program from a concert for a friend who might be interested in reading it.

- Leave a huge bunch of wild flowers at the back door when a friend is sick.

- Call a cousin you had a disagreement with and invite him to have lunch with you. You'll find you both will be grateful to be together.

- Give a friend a set of Filofax or Lefax diary refills or colored blank pages. Have some made with a friend's initials or first name printed in tomato red or Yale blue.

- "Do it now."

- Help a friend paint her apartment or pack and move.

- Put together a surprise gift box for each niece and nephew and send them out at once. These can be inexpensive items that they'll love from a novelty shop or a toy store.

- Buy your mother a book on a subject she loves or a record of her favorite music. Inscribe it with affection. Present this out of the blue; create your own special occasion.

- When good friends are moving out of town, plan a party for them with mutual friends.

- Start a ribbon collection and tie colorful ribbons on little gifts you give to others. Collect art shopping bags as gift stuffers for friends.

- Take a niece or nephew to a religious service.

- Remember that everyone is different. Most of us are doing the best we can.

- Buy some pastel cotton socks and give a pair to a friend. They're fun for exercising, keeping feet warm in the winter, and ideal for cozy days at home.

- Plan a family reunion for this summer.

- Try to think of something positive to say to the next person you're with, even when you're feeling blue.

- Include some of your favorite relatives in your next party. Arrange for them to stay at a nearby inn or hotel. This will be a treat for them.

- Plan a special event for the year 2000. Let your family visualize and anticipate what their life will be like then.

- Find your Dad's favorite cartoon and have it framed. Inscribe it and send it to him at his place of work. He can keep it on his desk and smile and think of you during a busy day.

- Share a fantasy or fear. You may find you're not alone.

- Telephone your parents (or favorite grandmother) every Sunday afternoon. Once this is a ritual it isn't difficult to remember. If you will be at a concert or on a boat trip and can't call, tell them in advance so they won't worry.

- Learn the words and tune of the hymn "Saving Grace." It will bring you peace.

- Nurture an attitude of gratitude and praise for others.

- If your family doesn't have a tradition of family gatherings, then start one. Each family can bring a dish, and you can alternate where you have it, each sister or brother taking a turn. Arrange these occasions ahead of time so everyone can mark their calendars.

- Once a week, get up an hour earlier and concentrate on doing things for friends. One week you might bake, another week write letters or poetry.

- Be a good listener. Your friend needs you to lend an ear.

- When geographical distance separates you and a family member and your life is extremely hectic, plan a visit when you can take a break from your work and the routine of life so you will feel refreshed, not exhausted, after the visit.

- Start a bridge group or have a poker party! Serve fresh fruit, cheese and crackers, finger sandwiches, and sparkling apple cider. Keep a stack of your favorite records playing.

- Write your family genealogy and learn your family history.

- When visiting your children, consider staying near them but not with them. This allows both of you to have some privacy and breathing space.

- Enjoy a zany, eccentric, artistic, colorful relative. Don't be embarrassed. They're adding some spark and zest to the world.

- Take the initiative and set something in motion with a relative. You are free to do things in your own terms and can create a positive environment.

- Make visits short and sweet.

- Pay a visit and chat. Just sit around the kitchen table and have coffee and gossip with your sister.

- Be flexible when unexpected events occur. You can be helpful and it will make you feel good.

- Invite a niece to have lunch with you so you can really get to know each other by being alone.

- Make a surprise phone call to a cousin and spend five minutes catching up.

- Sports buffs can rent a bus and have a road trip to a football game, baseball game, basketball, or hockey. Sing songs on the way. Have a tailgate party with covered dishes, bagels and cream cheese, champagne and orange juice, and coffee.

- Have a sense of humor.

YOUR
GRACE
NOTES

Unknown Others

"He liked to like people;
therefore people liked him."
—*Mark Twain*

Some of the happiest moments of my life have been unplanned. I can be sitting very peacefully at a beach, reading or writing, gazing into the water, and suddenly I may see a child collecting seashells or making a sand castle and I am swept away by sheer delight. I become one in my heart with that child. I love to observe the industry, the total absorption, and concentration. There is a glow of pleasure that a child radiates in all directions. The beach is as sweet as a birthday cake; it becomes a world of delight. I lose all sense of time and am carried away for this "moment of being" where I am enthralled.

A child is completely unself-conscious, oblivious to the pleasure I am receiving along with other sentimental observers. I am taken back to being on a beach at that age and I remember my brothers and sister and how much happiness we felt as carefree children playing at the water's edge. I remember my daughters at that age.

This surprise burst of joy can happen anywhere. I can read a book by an author I've never met and feel moved to tears knowing we're kindred spirits. I can get a thrill of joy when I hear children laughing or when I see an elderly couple defying time and kicking up their heels and having fun. These surprise occurrences—when

DELIGHTED—
BY CHANCE?

215

you are suddenly snapped out of your own preoccupation to focus on an unknown other and are transported—are the moments life offers to each of us. They are freely given gifts of joy.

These gifts are not accidents. They are reminders of the infinite possibilities open to each of us. Each day you awake to a new, changed rhythm and you can become a new person. Only you can do this for yourself.

You may have a tendency to ask yourself too many questions. Was I jealous that the little girl on the beach wasn't mine? Did I want to possess her? You may start thinking about how much work, time, and money it takes to raise a child—Those poor parents, you think—and soon the joy you felt from the encounter is gone. Sometimes the meaning of an experience is the experience itself, the feeling you have, the connecting of one person's spirit with another. What two people can learn from each other in a moment is meaning without need of explanation.

Wonderful serendipitous experiences happen to those who want them. It's that simple. Life is our stage where we can act out our parts. The ways you and I decide to program ourselves will bring what is going to happen to us. Have you ever awakened and thought, today is going to be a beautiful day? And it is. It's a kind of commitment to making the day beautiful that sends positive signals through the air.

Trust in the mystery.

ATTITUDE IS ALL

Positive personalities open their eyes and hearts to receive the good feelings of others. They are open to encouragement and all that is beneficial. Being part of the process of creating joy for an unknown other is an intoxicating tonic. You don't have to be an actor. Create your own performance for unknown others and you will connect. The hat you wear, your smile, your flowered dress, your pink socks, might delight strangers who see you on the street.

One way to connect is to reach out to someone you admire. I read the sweetest story about a doctor, George Schmieler. At seventy-one he had lost his wife of fifty years; on New Year's Eve he was "aching with despair" when he discovered a book his deceased wife had been reading—*I've Got to Talk to Somebody, God.* Marjorie Holmes, the seventy-year-old author, had also lost her husband of fifty years. He was so comforted by her words, he tracked her down through relatives and dialed her unlisted number announcing, "I love you. You saved my life." Holmes said his voice was "rich and pleasant" and she agreed to meet him, and nineteen weeks after they met they married. "We are convinced that this was the work of God. . . . If all men were like George, I doubt there would be unhappy marriages," says Holmes.

WRITE A FAN LETTER

If you read a book and feel close to the author, reach out and write a fan letter. The author will be pleased to know he or she has touched you. Be humble and tell the author how you were moved. We're not all writers, but a person who reads is of vital importance to the one who writes books. An author wants to know who the reader is and what were the most meaningful aspects of the book. Use the powers you have. An insecure person who says, "Why bother? Why would a famous author want to hear from me?" is hiding behind a feeling of powerlessness which is just another way of denying the possibility of connecting further. Remember, writers are extremely sensitive people who bare their souls for all time. You are saying to the author that you are sensitive too and you appreciate his greatness and beauty.

When exploring a relationship with an unknown other you may want to pick up a copy of the *I Ching* or *Book of Changes* and refer to the section called "Holding Together": "What is required is that we unite with others, in order that all may complement and aid one another through holding together," Confucius explains. "To bless means to help."

Every fan letter you write is like tossing another coin into the fountain—your wish may come true! If your effort at contact is not successful at first, then it may be later on. Or you may not get a response at all, in which case you've had the benefit of extending yourself—the way a dancer stretches to warm up so that the actual dance will be performed with ease. Your efforts and extensions will be an exercise of your humanness. No act of thoughtfulness will ever be wasted. They build to become part of your character.

René Dubos points out, "Our species acquires its humanness. . . . We are not born with the attributes essential for a truly human life but rather with potentialities that enable them to become human. We become human only to the extent that we take advantage of these opportunities."

Remember, reaching out to unknown others is part of your humanness, and your successes will be too.

A NEW DAY TO SMILE
Each day you can become a new person. Get out of bed with a smile on your face. Smile when you're alone, it's a good habit. You will be opening yourself up to greet unknown others in a life-enhancing way. A smile conveys and spreads joy. When I give a lecture and someone speaks with me afterward with a smile, I have a sense I've touched that person.

On your way to work look at the faces of the joggers, the walkers, the train commuters, or those stuck behind a steering wheel. You may find they are not exuding a lively joie de vivre. Try to spot the child skipping and swinging her lunch bucket holding her daddy's hand. She'll spread joy to you.

On days when you're feeling particularly good, look into the faces of others and smile, and see if someone notices you and smiles back. Usually a smile noticed generates a smile. A smile is a positive way of recognizing and confirming another individual.

You *can* change. Light up your face with a smile and let the positive energy charge the atmosphere around you. Look at people. Claude Monet taught us not to look at the surface of things, but into their depths. His last water lily series shows us what is under the surface of his Japanese-inspired pond at Giverny. Once you focus on a person, look beyond the surface and into the depth of the person's humanness. Go through your day observing others. Sense their character and notice their interesting faces. The French couturiere Coco Chanel rather irreverently stated, "Nature gives you the face you have at twenty; it is up to you to merit the face you have at fifty." Earn some laugh lines!

Unknown others will observe you. Cast your net widely and select people who interest you and edit out the others. Even if you never utter a word to a stranger and only share a smile and a glance, you have opened up inwardly and expanded. We really do wear our lives on our faces and without verbal communication we can respond to the body language of unknown others.

At dinner once two actress friends were arguing over Mikhail Baryshnikov's role in *Dancing*. One loved the body movements in a powerful way and the other didn't like his acting in the non-dancing part of the movie. Baryshnikov is a powerful dancer and many of us don't need to know how his voice sounds. We know him through his dancing—his body language is his strongest form of communication.

It is important to consider how much time Baryshnikov spent practicing his art so that he could communicate so poignantly and effectively. We all can learn to improve our physical communication by observing others and practicing. Stand in front of a mirror when you're alone and watch how you appear to others. Try to allow yourself to be as natural and clear in your expression as possible. Don't avoid looking at awkward photos of yourself—stare hard and see what you would like to improve. Maybe your hair needs combing more often than you thought, or you have a tendency to look down instead of at the others you're with. All of this can be altered in a natural way to communicate what you would like.

Ever since I traveled around the world as a teenager, I have overcome any embarrassment at not being able to speak every language where my travels lead me. I use my hands and I point, I smile, and I've always gotten along and had a good time. Language is only a part of communication. If we are open and aware and intuitive, we sense what is most important and what is real, and we can communicate that.

We all feel the pressures of living in such a dangerous time and are naturally guarded—we guard our privacy and our property. But remember the guard is the true prisoner; he will be there long after he releases the prisoners from their jail cells.

There are unknown others whom you can smile at in a crowded room and never see again. At another time, you could be on a cable car in San Francisco as a friend of mine was—he met and fell in love with a young woman sitting next to him and they've been married almost forty years! The way you look, the way you dress, your posture, the expression on your face, your voice, are telling a story to unknown others. Your own style and manner are communicating for you, sending signals to others. There are a whole lot of fascinating, charismatic people out there in the "lonely crowd" and the more you observe them and know about them, the richer your life will become.

OLD SOULS Have you ever met someone you immediately felt was an old soul? Someone you've known forever or before, in another life? I've read many books in which ministers and spiritual leaders account for these experiences—they are very real and inspiring.

I have a friend and counselor who says he's a "people, places, and things" person: "I understand here and now best." I laugh because it's true that we're all guests having a good time at the party of life, and for each one of us the party will someday be over. But while we're at the party we live through our physical presence with our senses, and we live passionately because we don't know when our stay will be over. We share this sense of the unknown.

I believe that as we move about together in a living world, we are deeply touched by some people we feel are kindred souls. The more we experience life's depths and sadness, the more we can appreciate being alive and healthy. We grow more attuned and sensitive, we learn to trust and live by our intuition.

The other day Brooke, a new freshman at college, was on the phone with Susie, a friend she'd known since kindergarten. Later she called Susie back to check on her (she had been ill) and there was no answer. She let the phone ring thirty to forty times knowing Susie was lying in bed next to the phone. "Maybe she's in the bathroom," Brooke thought. Suddenly she ran over to Susie's dorm and discovered her so weak she couldn't pick up the phone. She was rushed to the hospital and had her appendix removed.

We exercise this same kind of presence and intuition in all our relationships, as if it were a sixth sense. I believe we can actually will inspiring people to become part of us. I don't know the Roman Catholic missionary Mother Teresa personally, but I know of her and she is one of my unknown others. You don't always have to have physical contact with the unknown others in your life. You can add people to your private world by admiring them and being inspired by them. Mother Teresa believes, "Joy is a net of love by which you can catch souls. . . . We can do no great things—only small things with great love."

Who are some of the unknown others you look up to? Who are the people you don't know personally but greatly admire? Who are the superior men and women who have lived before you who have made significant contributions to your understanding and knowledge? Treasure these people who help guide your path.

Be on the lookout for other wise men and women in your midst. Each precious day we live we have the possibility to discover someone nearby who can change our lives and expand us. Think of the people you have met by chance who have added a spark of light and joy to everything you do, who have, through their own life and belief, guided you in your search. While you may not have someone who is literally divine in your radius, you probably have some people who are close to it!

Dwell on those whose example has been a gift of inspiration to you. Search for quality in the people around you.

"Just as the twig is bent the tree's inclined."
—ALEXANDER POPE

A GOD
WITHIN

One Sunday morning I went to a religious service at Lincoln Center with Mrs. Brown, who never became part of any church community but who, in her own words, "shopped around for a good sermon." She was taken with Dr. Butterworth, who preached at the Church of the Truth. On this particular Sunday Dr. Butterworth introduced his audience to a book entitled *A God Within* by the bacteriologist and Pulitzer Prize-winning philosopher René Dubos. I was so moved by his insights I remember taking out a little notepad from my purse and jotting down some phrases. I couldn't wait to read the book and on Monday I picked up a copy on my lunch hour. I began a real feast of pleasure with an unknown other. I didn't realize I knew anyone who personally knew René Dubos until much later.

I read *A God Within* as though I were on a voyage discovering a new country. Dr. Dubos was probably seventy-five years old when this book came out and I was about thirty. I can remember specifically how it happened that we met. Jim Morton, Dean of the Episcopal Cathedral in New York, was at our apartment at a cocktail party and he and I were talking. He was complimenting me on the apartment and I remember laughing, saying, "I have discovered a great thinker who has given me a new perspective about my work. Have you read René Dubos's book *A God Within*?" Jim smiled and asked me what I was doing Sunday. Dr. Dubos was preaching at the cathedral and was coming for lunch afterward. Would I like to join them with Peter? Would I! I was as excited as I ever remember being and truly felt that I must be dreaming a very good dream.

Because I mention René Dubos so often in my writing I am happy to report that we became friends after that meeting. We invited him with his attractive and intelligent wife Jean to our home for dinner and, you know what, they accepted! We quickly discovered many of our friends who were also admirers and put together a group of fans. So often when I dare to think I have made a personal discovery it is always a moment of humility to discover

I am not the first nor the last to admire the exceptional qualities of a person.

One time when Dr. Dubos and I were together he said, "Alexandra. It is all so simple. Men and women eat, they sleep, and they bathe. They stand up, sit down, or lie down. As a designer you think about these things and design accordingly." My book *Living a Beautiful Life* was based on our human functions of eating, sleeping, and bathing. When I am really stumped for a design solution I think of a man or woman standing, sitting, or lying down and I realize the solution to any problem comes from need and function. His chance words have proven endlessly useful for me.

I feel blessed that I "discovered" René Dubos, and I would like to share my discovery with you in his words:

"Even under the most favorable conditions, the maintenance of a healthy personality requires constant effort, because we all harbor many conflicting tendencies and depend for our survival on complex social relationships. Every perceptive adult knows he is part beast and part saint, a mixture of folly and reason, love and hate, courage and cowardice. He can be at the same time believer and doubter, idealist and skeptic, altruistic citizen and selfish hedonist. The coexistence of these conflicting traits naturally causes tension but is nevertheless compatible with sanity. In a mysterious way, the search for identity and the pursuit of self-selected goals harmonize opposites and facilitate the integration of discordant human traits into some sort of working accord."

Luck and timing play a big part in our discovering unknown others. I can pine away all I want and can't ever meet Cicero face to face! But I can admire his mind. I met Tom Wolfe when I went to a lecture on architecture and introduced myself to him afterward. I'd mentioned his book *From Bauhaus to Our House* in my book *Reflections on Beauty* and sent him a copy and he wrote to thank me. I first met one of my editors at a party. He asked me to let him know if he could ever be of help to me and gave me his card. I sent him a lengthy typed outline for my first book within the year. After discovering an artist's work and buying a painting I told the gallery owner I wanted to meet the artist, and did the next time he came to New York. I ended up having the artist and his wife as guests for our Thanksgiving dinner when they were in the United States on a visit.

SERENDIPITY

Unknown others are all around us. They are the wise people from history and they are the children on the beach. They are in the supermarket and on the street. They are in the emergency ward at a hospital and they are in their gardens. Some we will know only through books and movies, others we will hear speak or sing, or see dance or act, and we will be touched and changed and transported. Every day we have the opportunity to discover an unknown other who can become known to us and fill us with joy. We have to extend wide open to receive their many gifts, which often come in subtle disguises.

What magical serendipitous unknown other will become known to you today? What street corner, park, or busy place will have a seed planted there to help you to a deeper understanding of life's mysteries? Our goal should be "to burn always with this hard, gemlike flame," as Walter Pater wrote in the conclusion of *The Renaissance*, "to maintain this ecstasy is success in life."

GRACE NOTES

■ Write a fan letter to someone who has touched your life in a special way. It can be Oprah Winfrey, Tom Wolfe, or someone you've never heard of who wrote a good article.

■ Read *Letitia Baldrige's Complete Guide to a Great Social Life*.

■ Have a party and have the guest of honor be somebody you admire. Invite other admirers.

■ Know that today you are going to meet a very special person.

■ Become an avid people watcher.

- If you feel an affinity with someone, reach out and let them get to know you.

- Give kindness away freely.

- The more you give, the more your well is replenished. Give for the joy of giving—you'll find it really does feel good.

- When the spirit moves you, act. It might be a smile, or a pat, it might be handing someone a Kleenex at a funeral.

- Work to expand your peripheral vision. You'll live in a bigger world with many more possibilities.

- When you have connected with another person, keep your eye contact.

- Have calling cards made 2½ inches by 3½ inches with just your name on them. If you want someone to be in touch with you, you can write your number on it. This size is big enough for you to write a short note—about a book you would like to recommend or a product you think your acquaintance might appreciate, or whatever related to your conversation.

- When the spirit moves you, follow your instincts and pay a compliment to a total stranger.

- Everyone has a story. Discover the story in those you meet.

- Take a present with you wherever you go.

- Giving a present to the children of a new friend or even something for their pet will touch them.

- You can never have too generous a spirit.

YOUR
GRACE
NOTES

Book Mark

THIS BOOK WAS COMPOSED IN FOURNIER AND
BERNHARD MODERN BY PENNSET INC.,
BLOOMSBURG, PENNSYLVANIA

IT WAS PRINTED ON 70 LB STORA MATTE PAPER
AND BOUND BY THE ARCATA GRAPHICS/FAIRFIELD,
FAIRFIELD, PENNSYLVANIA

DESIGNED BY MARYSARAH QUINN

MARBLED PAPER PATTERN BY MARBLE EYES

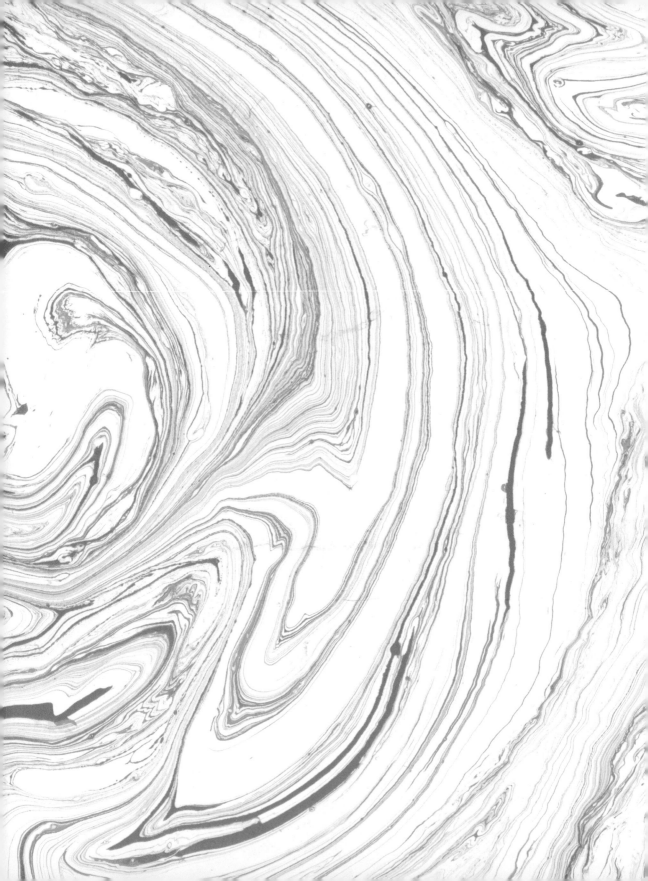